Dr Sophie Mort has a bachelor's degree in psychology, a masters in neuroscience and a doctorate in clinical psychology. Since 2018 she has helped thousands manage their emotional wellbeing by sharing her psychological expertise on Instagram, on her blog and through her online private practice. Sophie is an expert for the mindfulness app Happy Not Perfect and has been featured in global outlets including *Vice Magazine*, *Girlboss*, *Psych Central* and *Teen Vogue*. *(Un)Stuck* is her second book.

Praise for *(Un)Stuck*

'Put down your current book and start reading this. Dr Soph delivers with her deep knowledge and disarming approach. A great book that we could all learn from' **Dr Julie Smith**

'*(Un)Stuck* is a wonderfully crafted, highly accessible book for anyone who feels lost or trapped in a cycle they're struggling to break free from' **Joshua Fletcher (@AnxietyJosh)**

'This book will set you free to live a more intentional and fulfilling life' **Emma Reed Turrell**

'An utterly brilliant guide on how to break cyclical patterns that keep us stuck. This must-read by Dr Sophie Mort is no doubt going to change many people's lives. It has certainly made me want to put in the work to become (un)stuck! Read this book and learn from one of the leading names in the self-help industry' **Nicole Vignola**

'Sophie Mort has produced a wonderfully rich book, full of practical wisdom. Everything she says is grounded in understanding the hidden fears and subtle habits of mind that get us stuck in feelings of distress and disconnect. She brings her skills as a clinical psychologist to show, with clarity and compassion, how we can find freedom again' **Mark Williams, Professor Emeritus of Clinical Psychology, University of Oxford, and co-author of *Deeper Mindfulness***

Also by Dr Sophie Mort

A Manual for Being Human

Dr Sophie Mort

(Un)Stuck

Five steps to break bad habits and get out of your own way

GALLERY BOOKS UK

G

First published in Great Britain by Gallery Books,
an imprint of Simon & Schuster UK Ltd, 2023
This edition published in Great Britain by Gallery Books,
an imprint of Simon & Schuster UK Ltd, 2024

1 3 5 7 9 10 8 6 4 2

Simon & Schuster UK Ltd
1st Floor
222 Gray's Inn Road
London WC1X 8HB

www.simonandschuster.co.uk
www.simonandschuster.com.au
www.simonandschuster.co.in

Simon & Schuster Australia, Sydney
Simon & Schuster India, New Delhi

Important Note:
This book is not intended as a substitute for medical advice or treatment.
Any person with a condition requiring medical attention should
consult a qualified medical practitioner or suitable therapist.

A CIP catalogue record for this book
is available from the British Library

Paperback ISBN: 978-1-4711-9756-7
eBook ISBN: 978-1-4711-9755-0

Typeset in Bembo by M Rules
Printed and Bound in the UK using 100% Renewable
Electricity at CPI Group (UK) Ltd

MIX
Paper | Supporting
responsible forestry
FSC® C171272

To the people who no longer want to live their life on repeat and who are ready to take responsibility for their own happiness. You are courageous.

Contents

'Could the young but realize how soon they will become mere walking bundles of habits, they would give more heed to their conduct while in the plastic state. We are spinning our own fates, good or evil, and never to be undone. Every smallest stroke of virtue or of vice leaves its never so little scar.'

—WILLIAM JAMES

Introduction

*'Insanity is doing the same thing over and over
again and expecting different results'*
—ALBERT EINSTEIN

If Einstein was right, we are all insane.

Humans unwittingly repeat patterns day in, day out. We fall back into habits we so desperately try to kick. We engage in behaviours that actively get in the way of the things we want in life. We get stuck, living in a Groundhog Day of our own making but not necessarily of our own design.

There are reasons for this.

Sometimes we struggle to change our behaviour because change is hard and few of us have been taught about the psychology and neuroscience behind it, meaning we incorrectly believe change is driven by willpower and willpower alone.

Sometimes we repeat the same patterns intentionally, hoping for the best. You may be aware that you are doing something that needs to change – such as dating a person

1

who doesn't make you happy or working for a company that is draining all your energy – but you still don't change. You tell yourself, *I've been doing this for a long time, it's too late to give up now. Maybe it will suddenly get better, you never know.*

Sometimes we don't believe change is possible, so we don't even try. I know so many people who think, *This is just who I am, I will always be like this*, even though something really does need to change, like their habit of pushing friends away during their time of need.

News flash: no person is fixed. Our brains constantly adapt and remodel throughout our lives. Yes, this adaptation slows as we age – you and I will never be able to pick things up quite as fast as we did as toddlers or teenagers; that's normal – but the latest science shows that even when the brain starts to naturally lose some of its youthful vigour, it reorganizes itself in order to make the most of the resources it has. External factors like diet, exercise and other healthy lifestyle choices can keep our brains younger, healthier and more flexible.[1] You can indeed teach an old dog new tricks. Whoever you are, you *can* change . . . should you wish to.

More than 40 per cent of our actions are behaviours we engage in without conscious thought.[2] This means we often function on autopilot, and so we run the risk of sleepwalking through our own lives. Often it isn't until a good friend, mentor or therapist asks, 'Hmm, does it feel like this has happened before?' that the 'Oh yeah! This is a pattern for me' moments occur. Have you ever had that experience before? If not, I'm going to be that person for you, right now! Here are some questions to start us off.

Do you make yearly resolutions, start them with gusto, then

find that a couple of weeks down the road you have slipped back into your old ways? You want to go to the gym – you even have the time set aside – but sitting on your sofa feels so damn good. Your brain is simply saying, *I don't want to,* while another little voice chips in with: *What's wrong with you? You're a lazy failure.* A few days of this and it feels like your chance at change has gone for ever.

Or do you notice you continuously procrastinate when you have an extremely important task to complete, and the deadline is looming? Even when the work is something you want to do and actually care about?

·Or maybe you always date unavailable people, craving the affection of those who tell you from the get-go that they aren't really looking for anything serious?

Or perhaps you finally get a 'break' in life, like a pay rise or promotion, but instead of enjoying it, you start undermining yourself by acting in ways that would cause things to go wrong or finding ways to rain on your own parade.

Have you started to assume that this stuck feeling may just be part of who you are now? That you are destined to keep feeling tired and unmotivated to exercise or look after yourself better, to keep making bad decisions or argue with your partner? Do you beat yourself up, assuming most other people seem to live their lives like an arrow, shooting a straight line from intentional decision to action to outcome, while you feel like a river, meandering back and forth – or, worse, like a whirlpool going round and round in circles, teetering on the edge of being sucked under?

If you answered yes to any of these questions, relax; you are completely normal. Humans often go around in circles, even when we want to change. This isn't to say, *Don't worry about it, there are loads of reasons why it's okay to be stuck, so don't bother doing anything about it.* No! Knowledge is power, but action makes you powerful. This book will show you the 'whys' of stuckness and the 'hows' of getting unstuck. This book is about making change. In your life, your relationships, and potentially in the world, too.

As with all things psychology-related, this book is not a quick fix. Making meaningful change in your life is always a slow burn. I am offering you a roadmap to taking control of the direction of your life, but it is your job to put these ideas into practice on a daily basis.

This book will highlight the common areas of life where many of us are stuck on repeat, show you why these patterns occur and then help you to act in ways that will put a stop to these bad habits.

So, it's bye bye, Groundhog Day, and hello to the life you choose.

About me

Before we begin getting unstuck, I should really introduce myself. I'm Dr Sophie Mort, a clinical psychologist. I work with people who want to understand and manage their mental health and I'm a passionate believer in getting psychology out of the therapy room and into people's lives in ways that make sense to them. I wrote my first book, *A Manual for Being Human*, after an epiphany I had while driving away from a client appointment in 2018, when it suddenly dawned on me that people are rarely raised to understand themselves. Instead they are often taught to misunderstand the very normal experiences that make them human, which has serious consequences for their mental health. That moment led me to write the book that gave people the tools to understand and manage whatever stresses and strains they faced, without having to wait till they were in crisis or could see a professional in order to get this information.

My second book comes from a similar 'oh my god' moment during the first Covid-19 lockdown. On what felt like day 1,900 and something, but was probably only day 21, I read *The Top Five Regrets of the Dying* by Bronnie Ware (there's nothing like a global pandemic to get you thinking about your existence and the potential end of it). The top regret was: 'I wish I'd had the courage to live a life true to myself, not the life others expected of me.' This regret felt like a kick in the guts. The thought that some people's last words suggested that they felt they hadn't really lived, or at least not in the way they wished to, is hard to bear, isn't it? The next urgent thought was . . . how do I make sure I learn from this?

When I chatted to my clients, friends and family, I saw I wasn't alone in asking questions regarding how to live. Everyone was. Existential threats shake people awake; they make them look up from the rat race of life and ask what is important. Have I spent my life doing the right thing? What will I do when we are eventually allowed back into the world?

It is one thing knowing that we want to live a life that is true to ourselves, but seriously . . . how does one do that? For most of us it isn't as simple as saying, 'I am going to do it, I am going to be happy.' A bumper sticker or inspirational quote, no matter how nicely adorned or on trend the colour scheme, simply won't suffice when the going gets tough.

I work with courageous people all day every day, and this is why I know that more than courage is required to make meaningful change. When people seek out therapy they are often in crisis, and after a period of support, most learn to manage whatever it is they are going through and suddenly gain a new lease of life. There is often an urgent feeling of *Now I feel better I don't want to squander my time. I want to live the most fulfilling life I can find.*

When I first started practicing as a clinical psychologist, I assumed it would be as simple as supporting people to work out what they valued and helping them to carve out enough time in their day to do these things. But, as you will see in the examples littered throughout this book, and as I am sure you may have already recognized in your own life, it often isn't as simple as this. There can be so many barriers. Barriers that block you from getting to the starting line of trying something new and barriers that cause you to stumble and potentially fall before the finish line. When I thought about what I was seeing in my clinic, I realized I shouldn't have been surprised, as I too have navigated these seemingly circular paths.

This is what got me interested in researching all the ways we get stuck in our lives, and how to overcome them. It is what made me realize that there are five factors that people rarely fully understand that get in the way of us being able to take charge of our lives and stop going in circles. But it wasn't until that fateful day in lockdown that I considered collecting all the information I had gathered, with the intention of pulling it together into one book.

Most people assume that to live a life in line with their values they simply need to tackle their habits, and, indeed, that is where we will start in this book. But that is not the whole picture.

I already know that you have the courage to make change, as you wouldn't have picked up this book if you didn't dare to believe that your life could be different – better in some way. This book will walk alongside you through the next steps. It will give you a chance to learn from the regrets of the people who came before you by helping you decide on the life that is yours, not just the one you act out day to day. I won't say that this will protect you from having any regrets in your final hours – even if I put everything from this book into practice and successfully live a life I choose, I can think of at least one embarrassing drunken evening that I will still cringe at should I have the luxury of time to reflect on my life at the end – but I promise you this: this book will help you figure out what you want and what you are doing that gets in the way of achieving that. Then, it's up to you to put it into practice.

Ready? Let's begin.

Chapter 1

Habits

When working, civil rights activist and prolific writer Maya Angelou would wake up at 6 a.m. and head straight to a 'tiny, mean' hotel room she rented near her home. Her luggage consisted of a Bible, a deck of cards, a bottle of sherry and, of course, her writing materials. When she'd arrive at 6.30 a.m., she would lie across her bed, tucking her elbow into the fold of the sheets, and write until the first sherry break at 11 a.m. She'd then write again until lunch, when she would stop writing, go home and not look at the work again until 5 p.m. The next day, she'd start the same cycle over again. The room, at her request, was stripped of any decor before she arrived, and while she stayed, the sheets were never changed; only the bins could be emptied by the hotel staff, meaning that the environment was the same, day in, day out.

Some of the most important writers of our times have behaved in ways that might appear odd to us. Victor Hugo, author of *Les Misérables*, asked his valet to take all his clothes and not give them back to him until he had finished his manuscript, so that he couldn't possibly do anything else until he finished his work. And Herman Melville, the author of *Moby-Dick*, supposedly asked his wife to chain him to his desk while he wrote. I tell you these stories as they all relate to the ways individuals get stuck/unstuck.

Have you ever wondered how some people have high levels of self-control? How some people say they will do something, start it and stick to it, whether it be a new hobby or business venture? These people do not have a special secret genetic ability that the rest of us mere mortals do not.* No; researchers have shown that they simply set up their environments to avoid temptation. They work in silence, or in drab and uninspiring rooms, and because they are not fighting off competing attempts for their attention, they are able to focus.

Angelou created an environment that eliminated distractions that could derail her concentration. On top of that, she set up a specific environment that became associated with the task she wished to accomplish (in this case writing), meaning that any time she went into that specific environment, her brain registered the cue to write. Hugo and Melville, while it could be said that they did the same thing, never quite got the hang of creating situations in which writing could go smoothly without having to take extreme measures in the final weeks in order to get their work done.

While we might not want to be writers and we may not

---

* Unless you have ADHD or another neurodiversity that makes focus more of a challenge, without the right support.

have the luxury of hiring even tiny and mean hotel rooms, we could all learn something from Angelou, and even from Hugo and Melville. Why? It's all down to our habits.

What are habits?

Humans are creatures of habit. We live our lives on repeat, carrying out the same activities every day. We brush our teeth, we make our morning coffee, we get dressed. We do these things so often that even when we think we are doing them by choice, we are actually simply engaging in habitual patterns of behaviour triggered by a craving or something in our environment. If you are awake for approximately sixteen hours per day, you will on average only choose your actions for just over eight of them. This means that if you live until you are eighty, you might, if you are not careful, sleepwalk through thirty-two years of your life.

We weren't born with these habits, of course. As children, we had to be cajoled to brush our teeth before bedtime, even though we were no doubt way more interested in playing with our toys or our siblings for another ten minutes. It was enforced repetition that made this a daily routine that we didn't have to think about, saving us the mental energy of having to remind ourselves to do it twice daily (and hopefully a few emergency dental appointments too).

Habits are a good thing. William James believed that without habits we would only get one or two things done per day. Without habits, we would have to think about every single thing that we do, every second of our waking life, which would be time-consuming and exhausting. You can perhaps think of examples of this, like how hard you had to concentrate when you learned how to drive or how exhausted you were after a few days of studying for an exam. Learning requires more time and energy than your brain wants to expend, and it involves constant trial and error; like I said, exhausting.

People often say that it is not what we think but what we do that makes us who we are. If this is the case, for better or for worse, we are our habits. Thankfully, most habits not only save energy, but they are factually helpful. They are solutions to the problems we face in life. How do I wake myself up in the morning? Caffeine fix. How do I tackle germs? Wash my hands. How do I show this person I care? Smile. Habits are also how we multitask, such as holding a conversation at the same time as driving a car. Imagine what the roads would be like if we didn't manage to integrate all the necessary pieces of information required for driving – the rules of the road, how to perform manoeuvres, how to anticipate the behaviours and speed of others on the road – to the point where we know each of these things without conscious thought? It would be chaos.

Habits can also cause us to engage in dangerous behaviours. Have you ever reached for your phone while driving to quickly check a text, eyes on the words from your friend rather than on the road ahead? The habitual natures of driving and of looking at your phone make it seem like it isn't a big deal ... until one day, you look at your phone and the very worst thing happens.

Habits can be life-or-death-level important, but some

habits get in the way of us living the life we want and leave us feeling stuck. For example, many of us are so practiced at hitting the snooze button on our alarm clock that our hands now reach out from under the covers to silence the sound as if under someone else's control. We have no conscious awareness we are doing it, only realizing we have snoozed a million times when we wake with panic an hour later, pulling on our clothes and running out of the front door, extremely late for our first meeting of the day.

Our habits can be the difference between a life of ease, in which we move seamlessly between activities that we enjoy and those we must carry out, and a life that makes us feel stuck, like we are going in circles, with someone else sitting in the driver's seat. The problem is that creating new habits, and ditching bad habits, is challenging. It requires diligence and a deep understanding of how habits work.

Unsticking points

Have you ever had an 'aha' moment while reading a book but then struggled to summarize exactly what it was that you just read, even though you put the book down only moments ago? This is normal. If you imagine memory as having a bottle neck that only lets through the information that we either deeply value, have an emotional response to, or that we rehearse, it makes sense as to why we would lose information so rapidly. Even if we have an emotional response to what we read, there is often so much information that it is hard to pinpoint to your brain exactly which bits you should remember. Additionally, we often treat books as external hard drives, as we know we can return to look up a quote should we want it at a later date, meaning we don't engage in the processes that aid learning. To aid your recall of the information in this book, I will present you with key points that you can return to at regular intervals any time you feel a little stuck. For double memory points, get your highlighter pen out or turn over the corner of the page to mark the points that you wish to remember; it will help. So, here are your first unsticking points.

- Most of us believe that we decide how to act each day. We think we are choosing what to eat, wear and do with fresh eyes, but most of the time we act without thinking at all.
- The first step to getting unstuck involves identifying the habits we engage in that take us away from – and the habits we would need to cultivate in order to take us closer to – the person we wish to be.

Help, I'm stuck

'I didn't tell you about this the last time we spoke, but I've been trying and failing to stop drinking for so long. I don't think I'm dependent on alcohol, so I should just be able to cut it out, but I don't. I know why I started to drink – it was to manage the life events you and I talked about so many times in the past – but I feel like I've conquered the pain of those experiences, so it's not that that's keeping the drinking going. I know that stress is a trigger for my

drinking habits, and so I've tried to tackle my day-to-day stress using the breathing exercises and other coping strategies that usually work for me, but, like I said, I keep drinking. Thankfully I haven't told anyone I am trying to quit drinking, otherwise they would know how pathetic I am. What should I do?'

—An email from an ex-client of mine,
SAM, 30, who was wanting to restart therapy

Sam was a tech founder who lived in London. She was someone you would think was 'killing it' if their life achievements were listed in bullet points on this page. Lots of people told her this very thing the moment they met her, sometimes awe-struck, sometimes in voices tinged green with the envy they felt for her achievements. This kind of thinking made Sam miserable, as each new compliment only emphasized to her the mismatch between how she presented herself in the world and how she felt on the inside – the place where she felt a mess.

Sam had seen multiple therapists in her life: the first for anxiety; the second after a significant breakup; the third because she didn't like the second therapist and had looked for a replacement to help her tackle her heartache; and then, when she was twenty-nine, we started working together as her mood was low. In our sessions, she would swing from seeing her history of therapy as proof of her commitment to looking after herself and her ability to overcome difficulties in life, to seeing it as proof that she was broken. She would often do this, switch between feeling good about herself to flagellating herself, so we spent the sessions discussing both her drive and the self-flagellation she engaged in. We realized that the parts of her upbringing that led her to constantly undermine herself were also the parts that had caused her to thrive in the workplace. She was driven by a deep insecurity that caused her to need to climb higher and higher peaks in search of an accolade that would finally make her feel like she was enough. We spent two years working on both understanding her and finding ways forward. Then one day she felt ready to go it alone. She felt braver in herself, understood her stresses and strains and how to cope alone. It was a proud moment.

A year later, I got the email asking to start work again to help her stop drinking. The quote above is taken directly from that email.

When we met for an assessment session, a number of things came to light. Firstly, she believed that most people turn to alcohol as a coping mechanism, and therefore if you wanted to stop drinking you needed to address the underlying issues, otherwise stopping drinking would either be impossible or would lead her to switch to a new coping mechanism, which could be even harder to stop. I agreed. Secondly, she knew that stress triggered her drinking, so she had worked on that, but the drinking continued. *Why am I still drinking?* she wondered. Was there still some underlying, unresolved pain that we hadn't arrived at yet that was causing her to drink?

As a therapist, I spend the majority of my life asking people to get curious about what might underlie certain behaviours that arise for (seemingly) no obvious reason. Sam had, across her lifetime, had four therapists ask her to do just this, and she was now a whiz at it. I was immediately up for the challenge. What could be going on? Was she secretly struggling with something that she was yet to be aware of? Was it social anxiety? The ideas flooded in.

Writing my client notes later that day, I considered these words of Abraham Maslow: 'If the only tool you have is a hammer, it is tempting to treat everything as if it were a nail.' I used to have this quote written on a Post-it note on my desktop computer when I worked in the NHS. It was there to remind me that sometimes, as a therapist, you may assume everything has a deep psychological meaning, when actually there is something quite different going on. Sam, like almost every person I meet who tells me they feel stuck, wanted to kick an old habit, and believed that, as long as she had addressed the underlying causes for a behaviour, she should be able to change that behaviour simply because she had decided to. Sam was a classic case of falling into the willpower trap.

Researchers are still unsure exactly how willpower works. Up until recently, it was considered to be a finite resource which, like petrol in a gas tank, will at some point run out, leaving you with nothing to use for the next task (i.e. if you concentrate on a difficult task for a few hours, then that evening you will find your willpower has run out and you can no longer resist temptation). More recent studies have shown that this theory is inaccurate, and that telling ourselves our willpower is finite means that we're more likely to give up the moment we start to feel tired.[1] Some researchers suggest it can be helpful to think of willpower the way we think about emotions, in that it ebbs and flows. We have willpower only some of the time, so when it is here, we should use it, but we cannot bank on it.

Also, motivation tends to follow action – kicking in once we see the fruits of our labour – rather than preceding it.

How many times have you relied on willpower to get you out of a slump? To get off the sofa and get to the gym? To stop texting the ex that you know isn't good for you? To ignore the other internet tabs that are infinitely more interesting than the Zoom call you are on? To pull away from the person who isn't your partner, whose lips are hovering above yours, when it would be easy just to say, 'Fuck it'? And how many times has this not quite worked out?

Sam hadn't relied on willpower alone, though, had she? She had addressed the root cause of her drinking. She had also done something else that was very smart and should not be overlooked. She, like Angelou, had realized there were some situations (in Sam's case, anything that triggered stress) that could stop her from attaining her desired goal and she had addressed them. However, she had not done a full Angelou and stripped away all the other cues that triggered her drinking habit . . . and this was the problem.

Not telling anyone about her plan meant that her housemates had no idea of the temptation they posed while they passed wine around the dinner table. Sam, like many people, didn't realize that when a behaviour is habitual it is triggered automatically by visual cues from our environment as well as internal cues (physical sensations and experiences). She didn't realize that stress was not the only cue for her drinking; cues were absolutely everywhere. Stress, the end of work, seeing certain friends, the route home, the kitchen, the dinner table – all made her want to drink. And that meant that, more often than not, the cravings won.

There was no deep and as-yet-unrealized psychological cause for the drinking. It wasn't that she was weak-willed, which was her other theory for her current situation. The issue was that she had not changed her environment. She was like a gambler trying to kick their habit while still sitting in the casino.

The first thing Sam and I worked on involved learning about willpower and the science of habit formation. Let's get into that science now so that you can avoid the traps Sam faced.

How habits are formed

I met Annie and John during my first days working as an assistant psychologist in a nursing home back in 2012. They were both in their eighties, and Annie had Alzheimer's while John had cognitive impairment following a severe stroke. Annie was sweet, chatty and dishevelled; John, aloof and contained. Neither of them could tell me the names of their grandchildren or what they had eaten that day, and I naively thought that they had lost all sense of who they were.

Over the following weeks I started to notice that, at intervals throughout the day, Annie would check on other residents, asking if they were okay and fetching them things like mugs and towels. As for John, at 8.30 every morning, he would be smartly dressed, with a random assortment of papers in hand, walking purposefully to the door. I was too inexperienced to know what was going on, so the staff at the home filled me in. Annie had been a ward nurse and John had been the proud CEO of a company. They could no longer remember recent events, but their habits were deeply entrenched.

Each time you repeat an action, it's the equivalent of walking over the same patch of earth and putting your feet directly into your old footprints. By the time your action becomes a habit, it's the equivalent of treading a worn path through a landscape. When you consider that you have been laying down neural pathways like this since you were born, creating deeper grooves and ravines with each repetition of behaviour, you can see why habits become so ingrained and hard to step out of. You're basically a Grand Canyon of habits.

What your habits look like:

Cue (something you see or feel)

↓

Urge (that you may or may not even be aware of)

↓

Habitual behaviour

↓

Resolution (desired outcome achieved)

An incredible thought: many of your habits will be with you until the day you die. This is the reason people say, 'It's as easy as riding a bike.' You can spend years away from a previously habitual behaviour and pick it up as if it was only yesterday that you were pedalling safely towards your intended destination.

A terrible thought: many of your habits will be with you

until the day you die, even when they harm you or you no longer enjoy them. That is, if you don't actively take time to change them!

Once a habit is deeply ingrained, it will keep going whether you want it to or not. Even when people no longer get a rush from smoking, they will still reach for the nicotine hit. This is the true sign of a strong habit: an action that is not perturbed by a lack of motivation.

It is important to note that the longer you have engaged in any habit and the more emotionally important the experience is for you, the more cues you will have to trigger that action, as everywhere you go and everything you do around the time of the habit becomes associated with it. Have you ever broken up with someone you were dating for a long time and noticed that everything you see and do reminds you of them? A song, a café, a sunny morning, a rainy evening, a joke they would have laughed at, a comment that would have made them roll their eyes? It makes sense to us that this would happen, because that person is associated with every part of our life, yet when it comes to our habits, we often don't think the same way. We don't realize how many aspects of our lives trigger our patterns.

For Sam, this meant that she needed to become much more aware of the cues that were triggering the behaviour she wanted to quit so that she could start removing them from her life. When applying what you have learned from this book to your life, you need to get curious about the cues that you could be missing that trigger the behaviours you want to ditch, so that you can get ahead of them going forward.

Identify your habits and cues

- **Get aware:** a core skill that will help you identify and overcome all the factors discussed in this
book is mindful awareness. The STOP technique
is a quick and easy way to practice this. To do it:
set an alarm on your phone at multiple intervals
throughout the day. When it goes off, or if you
notice a strong sensation or emotions, **s**top what
you are doing, **t**ake three breaths, **o**bserve your
emotions and ground yourself in the room, then
choose how you want to **p**roceed, having given
yourself a moment to relax. Alternatively, you could
ask yourself when the alarm goes off, 'What am I
doing right now? Why am I doing it? Is this what
I want to be doing?'
- **Use this to get aware of your habits and cues.**
Spend the next forty-eight hours paying careful
attention to the actions you engage in repeatedly.
What happened just before you did that thing?
What did the urge to complete the task feel like?
Were you even aware of the trigger, or did you
find yourself doing the task? How did you feel
afterwards? Can you spot the habit loop we learned
about above? No need to write anything down;
we will do that later. Simply pay attention to
your actions.

Unsticking point

- The life-long endurance of habits is both a strength and a curse. It means that when we develop new habits, we are not wiping out the old ones and replacing them. We are creating new pathways that we need to build environments to support.

Good vs bad habits

People talk about 'good' and 'bad' habits. These terms can be helpful when we strip away the moral judgement assigned to 'good' and 'bad' and instead think of them in terms of how they affect our lives, with good habits describing the behaviours that are in line with, and take us closer to, the people we would like to be in the future, and bad habits describing the actions that divert us from our goals.

Excessive alcohol consumption is usually deemed a bad habit, and for Sam it really was affecting her life. However, having a drink once a day may be a pleasurable pastime that never harms you, whereas procrastinating when confronted with an important task may be extremely detrimental to your future. That's right: for some people, procrastination is a more destructive habit than alcohol. It may not feel like that in the moment; how bad can checking your phone be instead of doing your work? It might not sound that bad, but what if you do that for ten minutes today, then ten minutes tomorrow, and every day for a year? That's 3,600 minutes, or sixty hours – over seven eight-hour working days spent procrastinating.

Humans are not good at seeing the big picture or the cumulative effects of small actions. Put a frog in a pan of cold water and slowly turn the temperature up, one degree at a time, and the frog won't notice it is being boiled alive until it's too late. A horrible image, but, unfortunately, we can all be a bit frog-like when it comes to putting off starting a new habit.

The procrastination habit loop

**Think about doing something new/
strenuous/complex**

↓

Feelings of discomfort arise (cue)

↓

The urge to avoid the feelings arises (urge)

↓

**The thought of *What's one more day? I will
do it tomorrow* or the action of reaching
for another activity arises (response)**

↓

Feelings of discomfort are removed (resolution)

Nathanael Emmons, the influential eighteenth-century American theologian, said, 'Habit is either the best of servants or the worst of masters,' and I have to say, procrastination is a cruel mistress. She lures you in with the promise of more joy, more fun and time away from the laborious tasks at hand. However, the joy and fun don't prevent your tasks from looming overhead.

For many of us, 'bad' habits develop because we're looking for a quick fix. The snooze button, the phone scroll, the Netflix binge: all more pleasing activities in the moment than whatever boring or strenuous task you are really meant to be doing. And, as you know, the longer we engage in any habit, the more cues become associated with that action, making it hard to get away from. For example, maybe you scroll on social media or watch TV to unwind at the end of a long day, and now you notice you start thinking about your phone or TV any time you feel stressed, bored, confused, irritated or tired. Suddenly you find yourself prioritizing looking at screens instead of getting your work done, meaning that the quick fix often ends up taking over hours of your life, slowly undoing your ability to achieve your daily tasks.

If you are reading this thinking, *Oh god, I do that*, me too. We all do it. Shaming yourself is not the solution to behaviour change; it is usually a one-way ticket to more misery! So, stop the negative self-talk (another bad habit!) and stay with me, as by the end of this chapter you will know what to do. And for those of you who think your procrastination is more than simply a habit, Chapter 3 is going to help you figure out what truly underlies your self-defeating behaviour.

Getting to know your good and bad habits

1. **Ask yourself:** are you feeling stuck because you are struggling to start good habits, or because bad habits are getting in the way of you being able to be who you want to be? It's likely to be a little bit of both, as it is often the bad habits (such as putting things off to tomorrow or overfilling your schedule) that make creating better habits impossible.

2. **Consider the kind of person you wish to be in the future.** If you don't already have a clear sense of this, turn to the values exercise on page 93 in Chapter 2. Head to Appendix 1 and answer the initial questions and fill in the first two columns. Do not skip this. This exercise is extremely important for creating good habits, because motivation arises from our identity. I am motivated to write this book as I am a psychologist who shares information. I am not motivated to chase people down in the street for their misdemeanours as I am not a police officer. Write down what values the person you wish to be has and would like to live by.

Not all habits are created equal

So far, we have learned that habits are built to achieve a resolution (e.g. completing a task or distracting us from a bad feeling). This is true, but there is more to it than that. Sometimes the resolution is a neurochemical or an actual reward, like the buzz of nicotine hitting your brain, feeling butterflies in your stomach when your crush smiles at you, or receiving a promotion at the end of a challenging project.

When it comes to rewards, intrinsic rewards such as satisfaction, a sense of purpose or a significant change in mood are a greater predictor of new habits than external rewards like money. The bigger the reward, the faster you will learn to crave it and therefore repeat the activity.

Anita, a client of mine with a go-getter spirit and penchant for to-do lists and life hacks, started having panic attacks, which made her feel like she was going to die or 'go utterly mad' – a feeling anyone who has had a panic attack will know all too well. Immediately, she slipped into action, devouring the online blogs tackling anxiety, trying breathing and grounding exercises and other scientifically backed coping skills. No matter what she tried, however, the panic did not subside.

When she came to therapy, I was impressed by how bravely she had thrown herself into finding ways to overcome the panic. As someone who has had panic attacks, I know how terrifying they are, and how all I wanted to do after they started was to crawl into bed and have something or someone else take the pain away.

Anita had done all the right things; she simply had not done them enough – trying one, finding it 'didn't work', then moving to the next. I say this without judgement, as the first time you try skills like this, the symptoms tend to intensify, as you start to focus on sensations that you usually desperately ignore. The alarm bells get louder. It feels like your brain is screaming at you, telling you that you are trying to put out an oil fire with water, and that you must stop immediately lest you want your whole metaphorical house to burn down. This is not the case. So long as what you are dealing with really is anxiety, these exercises really are at least part of the solution. However, as I explained to her, they must be practiced as if your life depends on them, until they become so habitual that you can slip into them the moment you need help to decrease your anxiety.

She struggled at the beginning. It was an effort to remember to do the breathing exercises and she didn't notice a significant improvement right away, so there was no rewarding response to drive her towards creating the new habit. Nevertheless, she persisted. She supported her to-do list by setting notifications on her phone to cue her to do the exercise five times a day. Then, one day, she practiced the breathing exercises and the panic immediately subsided. The rush of relief (the intrinsic reward) that she experienced prompted her to practice harder and harder until relaxation rolled in almost the instant she slowed down her breath. It took time and practice before the intrinsically rewarding sensation arose and became paired with the activity, but once it had, the reward got stronger, arose quicker, and the habit took hold. This is what I meant earlier when I said that motivation often follows, not precedes, action.

Never one to miss an opportunity to increase efficiency, a month or so later, Anita told me that she applied what she had learned to another area of her life. She was self-employed and continuously behind with invoicing her clients. She found that no matter how many reminders she set for herself, she would sometimes ignore the reminder and invoicing never became habitual. 'Why?' she asked. 'You'd imagine a cash incentive would be enough to make this into a habit.'

There are many issues arising here, but the time clients took to pay up (often at least a month passed between invoicing and receiving money) meant she never clearly associated the reward with the action. Because there was no identifiable, immediate reward, invoicing remained an effortful routine she carried out only when her bank balance got low, jolting her into action.

To change her behaviour, we decided that instead of trying to make invoicing a habit, she could set up a weekly account-ability call with her friend who also hated invoicing and make a rule that they would tackle their most boring tasks first – which for both was, you guessed it, invoicing. Over time, tackling their most boring task first became second nature. That was how she overcame her invoicing problems. She set up what Charles Duhigg, author of *The Power of Habit,* calls a 'keystone habit': one that acts as an overarching theme with a direct effect on all other behaviours. Other examples of key-stone habits include practicing honesty, as this has a knock-on effect on all of your relationships; making a detailed plan for your day when you wake up, as this organizes your thoughts and priorities for the next twenty-four hours; and regularly meditating, as this affects your overall mood and resilience.

The bottom line of habits: if a task feels manageable and gives you a powerful enough kick of reward that is close enough to the time you enact the behaviour, you are likely to be able to habitualize it ... at some point. Sorry to be the bearer of bad news, but the range of time it takes to create a habit is usually between two and a half weeks to nine months.[2] Like I said, speed of acquisition is linked to many factors, including the simplicity of the task, how regularly you practice said task, and how much of a reward you gain from the task. But then some stuff – like invoicing – is just tedious, and sometimes we just must get on and do hard things.

Unsticking point

- You need to know what you find personally rewarding. You and I likely don't have all the same habits, as we won't always find the same things rewarding. A good rule of thumb for all habits is that they will arise most quickly when the reward feels significant and instantaneous.

Big hitters

Unfortunately, many of the things in life that give us the fastest and strongest rewards are not that good for us in the long run. Drugs like codeine, cocaine and heroin are so addictive because the biological hit your body receives is so strong and so immediate that habits can start to form within a matter of days. Particularly when the reward you receive is not only biological but also a release from loneliness, fear and grief – many of the serious and hidden drivers behind addiction.

If we regularly use substances such as cocaine or alcohol, we are not only likely to become dependent, but we can also experience DNA changes, such as the removal of our natural genetic brake that usually constrains our ability to create habits.[3] This means we are predisposed towards habitual actions going forward. If this is you, don't worry; the tips from this book still apply to you. You can still create new, healthy habits and move away from the ones that have got you stuck right now, but you may need to be more vigilant about planning your way to unsticking yourself. Should you need professional help, there are addiction support teams set up to help with exactly this.

Drugs aren't the only big hitters these days. 'Bigger and better' hits are everywhere. A tonne of crisps is consumed every four minutes in the UK, and McDonald's serves 3.8 million people per day.[4] These numbers are so high because the food is created to hijack our reward centres. Crisps are manufactured for crunch (research shows the louder the crunch the more people will eat) and speed of flavour delivery, so you get a chemical hit the instant you pop a crisp in your mouth. Likewise, McDonald's chips are manufactured to disintegrate in your mouth in a millisecond, mainlining salt to your taste buds faster than non-processed foods ever could. The reward is as instantaneous as the bite.

Have you ever wondered why people don't lose control around celery or even a good steak in the way so many (myself included) do around crisps and McDonald's? This is because natural items were not designed to hook us in.

Celery doesn't care if you eat it, and the cow would seriously prefer it if you didn't! They don't exist for us. Whereas food producers really care; if we don't want their items, they don't make money.

We all know how addictive nicotine is, but when you inhale a cigarette it can take 6–10 seconds for neurochemical changes to occur. Pop salt or sugar on your tongue and it only takes around eight tenths of a second.[5] The moment many of us see a crisp packet or the golden arches, our habit gets triggered and, like zombies, we start moving towards the precious foods.

Industries succeed when they can hijack our cravings. Fast food, social media and porn are the fastest hits in town. The most likely to get you hooked. The most likely to make you feel dissatisfied with real food, real people, real sensuality and sex, all of which simply can't elicit the same hits. They're also the most likely to be backed by large companies pouring millions into making that hit even faster in the future so that we will choose their product over others.

The confusing thing about rewards is that we are more powerfully motivated by unpredictable rewards than consistent rewards. This is why social media is built to intermittently reinforce your behaviour with likes and saves, which are out of our control. This is why most of us think we are more attracted to the person who texts us then disappears, popping back up without warning.

In short, sometimes we are stuck because we have developed habits of our own choosing that get in the way of what we want to do in life; other times, they arise outside of our control. When we truly understand what habits are and how they work, we can recognize that most things we consider distractions in life – like checking our phones, getting derailed by the snack aisle in the supermarket, online shopping instead of doing work – are not distractions *per se*, but are the environment or our internal states (such as boredom or hunger), triggering habits that we weren't intending to engage in. I tell you this firstly as I want to ensure you offer yourself compassion around the habits that you aren't necessarily pleased about; and, secondly and most importantly, to drive home the point that we must consider our environment (the cues and the rewards it offers) when we decide to change our habits.

A special note for people who are engaged in habits that they hate but carry out anyway: don't get disheartened if you notice a habit that you hate but still engage in.

As we have learned, strong habits can continue even when we don't enjoy the action anymore. So, what do we do?

We use mindfulness to pay attention to the actual experience of the habit we don't want to engage in anymore, so that over time new associations are made with the activity. Let's use smoking as an example. If you want to quit smoking, pay attention to the experience when you find yourself smoking. How does your mouth feel when you smoke? How does your head feel? How do you feel afterwards? Start collecting evidence without judgement. Do you actually enjoy it? Or does it make your chest feel tight and your head swim? Keep a record, and notice how, over time, your brain slowly starts to associate the cue and craving with an afterthought of, *Hang on . . . maybe I don't want to do that thing after all.* This is a slow process, but it works.

Addressing the bad and bringing in the good

- **Return to Appendix 1 and complete column three, the cues that cause your bad habits to arise.** Is it boredom causing you to reach for your phone? Loneliness? The fact that it's in front of you? Is it a physical sensation of fatigue that causes you to stay sitting on the sofa instead of getting to your next activity? Or the fact that once your episode is over, Netflix automatically starts the next? List all the cues you can think of. Go through the list and circle any cues you can remove from your environment and make a note of how you will do this (e.g. if you keep texting the ex you know is bad for you, is it time to delete their number?).

- **In column four, write down what reward or resolution may be keeping each habit alive.** Is it the relief you experience after giving in to the urge to do that thing? Is it the removal of another emotional state?

- **In column five, list activities you could engage in that would meet that resolution.** These may end up being your new replacement habits. People who go to Alcoholics Anonymous are assigned a sponsor so that they have a new behaviour to engage in the moment a craving starts, which is someone to call. What will you do to meet your new needs? **Do not skip this!** Writing down our planned actions increases the likelihood of reaching our goals by 42 per cent.[6] And, perhaps more importantly, when we try to remove a habit without replacing it, we set up a situation in which 1) we are most likely to get stuck in a *Will I do it? Wont I do it?* battle in our heads, which often leads us back to the bad habit simply because we want to quieten the mental noise; 2) we remove potential safety nets without offering alternatives (remember, many bad habits are there to alleviate an emotional state such as loneliness, grief and fear), causing us to be tempted to reach for something stronger to manage the mood later on; 3) we miss out on the opportunity of leveraging an already present habit loop (i.e. a behavioural pattern that has a cue and an outcome). So, please, give the exercise a go.

- **In column six, write any additional 'good habits' you wish to develop going forward, and in column eight, how you are going to reward these new behaviours.** Consider extrinsic and intrinsic rewards. For example, as well as rewarding yourself with coffee with friends after exercise, focus on how the behaviour is going to make you feel after the event. Will going for a run make you feel smug? Will it mean you can have a lie-in tomorrow? Before each repetition of your new behaviour, say to yourself: 'I am going to do [insert the activity] and afterwards I will feel [insert either the reward you gain from this activity, the feeling it will give you, or how it will contribute to your future self]'. In fact, when you add the activity to your diary, add the way you will feel to the title of the event.

- **After you have been doing your activity for a while, plan intermittent rewards.** For example, if you are running with a friend, take it in turns to decide what the after-run activity is, and on occasion agree that it will be nothing, but that you (the person who doesn't know) won't be told until that event happens.

- **Do not reward yourself before you start your new activity.** I know it is tempting to do this – I sometimes look at puppies on Instagram before I sit down to write, or I take myself for a nice coffee beforehand to get me in the mood. The issue here is that starting a task already hopped up on dopamine means that even if your new activity feels rewarding, the hit won't be significantly different to how you already feel, meaning it won't get you hooked. Remember, cocaine gets people hooked because the reward is stronger than anything we can create ourselves. Don't starve yourself of joy, but give your activity a chance to give you a boost first.

Repetition and getting it wrong

Let's go back to my time with Annie and John. Even though Annie's Alzheimer's and John's stroke had left them with limited memory, they carried out old habits like getting up early and helping others around them, and they also engaged in new activities that had been learned since entering the home. I was astonished. How was this possible? Surely, we must need memory to pick up new habits? No!

Some of the people in this home were learning to dress themselves and find their way to their local shop through a process called errorless learning (fancy talk for teaching someone a skill step-by-step, stopping them just before a mistake is made). It worked because different parts of the brain are responsible for habit and memory – as long as the areas associated with habit were intact, habits could be learned. Repetition was key.

When researching this book, I listened to a Huberman Lab podcast in which the host, Andrew Huberman, associate professor in the Department of Neurobiology at Stanford University, discussed an example so unusual that I thought about it constantly after hearing it. Researchers have known for a long time that if they put two mice in a tube, one will push the other out. They also know that the mouse they should put their money on is either the one that is most dominant and strong, or the one that just won the previous challenge (winning gives animals of all kinds a boost to try harder and win again next time). In 2017, however, researchers found that there was another way to make a winner, irrespective of the size and testosterone levels of the animal, or whether it had won or lost on the previous round, and that was by stimulating the dorsomedial prefrontal cortex. This is the area of the brain that is involved when deciding how much effort to put into a task based on a cost–benefit analysis.[7] In the experiment, the researchers put a group of mice in a small space with only one warm corner, heated by a lamp; the rest of the floor was ice cold. They found that the mouse whose dorsomedial prefrontal cortex had been stimulated routinely got closer to the heat lamp than any of the others. This brain stimulation hadn't made the subject into a super mouse, it simply increased the mouse's perseverance. It wasn't stronger than the other mice; it merely made more attempts to reach its goal than any of the others.

You are not a mouse trying to reach a heat lamp, but you are a human who, if you are anything like me, may have less strength and stamina than you think you need in order to achieve your desired goals. If that resonates, you now have the first trick to success in your hand: repeat your new action again and again, resist against pushback, and you will get there.

Remember I said a little earlier that repeating a habit is like walking across fresh grass? Let's continue this analogy, but this time I want you to imagine you are in a field full of really tall crops. In the middle of the crops, there is a path (this represents your old habit). This path exists because you have walked it over and over again, trampling the crops, grinding them down so that there is a clear walkway through the field. You decide not to take this path; instead, you want to take a different route. You set off into the tall crops, but it's hard. Maybe you give up because the resistance from the crops is so strong, and the urge to head back to the old path is even stronger. Maybe you struggle through, noticing how much more effortful this route is and how much quicker you tire.

If you make it to the other side, well done! Full marks. Now, imagine the path you left behind. Is it visible? How does it compare to the path you normally take? The answer is that the new path is barely visible compared to the old one, but there is some trace of it. You could find it again if you looked for it, but it would be hard.

This is a simplified version of what we do every time we try to change a habit. We come up against resistance. We tire more quickly, and as soon as we are tired, we are more likely to give up. So, when we only engage in a new behaviour a few times, the procedural memory is created but no habit is even close to being built.

Think about how many times you have set a new year's resolution, carried it out for a few weeks and then given up. Or how regularly you have set yourself a goal, like exercising before a holiday or a triathlon, and then stopped the moment the goal has been achieved. Consider how often you have wanted to stop spending money or drinking too much and found yourself back at it following a few days of abstinence. This is normal and can be overcome through persistence.

Fun fact: habits are more quickly acquired if you focus on creating an 'instigation habit' than an 'execution habit'.[8] In plain speak, this means the impulse to initiate a new action is more important than what you do during the action. For example, if you want to start going to the gym, creating as many cues as possible that trigger the impulse to exercise – such as getting your gym kit ready and laying it next to your bed so it is the first thing you see when you wake up, or booking a class in advance – is more important than what you do when you get to the gym. Focus more on how you are going to get yourself to do that activity than what you will do when you are there. With this in mind, return to Appendix 1 and complete column seven: 'what cues you will add into your environment to get your actions going'.

Caution: if you start too many habits at once or leave gathering all the items necessary for your habit till the moment you plan to start the habit, you are setting yourself up to struggle. Introducing too many new activities will exhaust you quickly due to the effort of holding all of your new plans in mind at once. And, if you don't have all the ingredients you need already in place for your new habit and have to run to the metaphorical or actual supermarket at the last minute, you may notice this additional step is the barrier that makes you think, *I can't be bothered, I'll start tomorrow* . . . Make your new habit so easy to engage in that you don't have to give it much thought at all.

If you are reading this at the end of the day and have suddenly realized that you have forgotten to repeat a task you are trying to turn into a habit, put the book down and simply visualize doing the task you were meant to do in the exact order you would do it. If it was washing your face (no judgement on your grubbiness), imagine going to the sink and turning on the tap, lathering up the cleanser and applying it to your skin. Your brain does know the difference between reality and imagination, which means that visualization will never replace action, but it will nonetheless help to activate important receptors in the brain, and the core process necessary for learning will be initiated, making the task easier to repeat again tomorrow.

The most common barriers to repetition

- **Ask yourself:** what has got in the way of being able to repeat activities to the point of them becoming habitual in the past? Write the reasons down. What can you do to overcome these barriers in future?

As I don't know what your answers will be, here are the most common reasons that you are struggling to start a new, good habit.

1. **You did not create a plan.** Luckily, this won't be you going forward! If you have been doing the exercises I have given you, you are well on your way to overcoming this common pitfall.
2. **You did not make time for the changes you need to make in your diary.** How many times do I meet people who plan to go to the gym five times a week when they already barely have time to sleep? Or who say, 'I will do it today', and then find that by the end of the day they still haven't done it? We have to clearly schedule our new activities into our diaries (but before you do this, wait until you have read to the end of this chapter to find out when it is best to schedule certain activities).

---

3. **You were not specific enough about what you wanted to do.** Break down your activity into small chunks. For example, if you are creating new habits around work, state what you will do each day. Rather than 'work on my business', say you will 'complete blog post on X' or 'send outstanding invoices'. Then say exactly when you will do it, e.g. 'I will send outstanding invoices when I first sit down at my desk. After that, I will complete my blog post on X.'

4. **You did not start small enough or started so small that it was boring to you.** Do you floss one tooth or floss the whole mouth? Do you start with a five-minute run or go straight in for thirty minutes? The science tells us that we learn fastest when we engage in tasks we can accurately complete 85 per cent of the time.[9] And the science tells us that we are more likely to succeed at doing something if we have already succeeded at something. If a mouse wins a competition, it is more likely to win the next, too, and in our case, the boost of completing something on our to-do list can motivate us to do another thing.

5. **You did not bring other people in on the action.** Don't do it alone. Find people who share your vision, or who are quitting the same bad habit or taking up the same activity. Not only will attending a group like this increase accountability,

but it will also bolster the sense of identity you are working towards and make the habit more enjoyable and likely to be sustained. Head to Appendix 1 now and complete column ten.

6. **You didn't pick a keystone habit – a single action or rule that has wide reaching effects – and instead chose multiple small habits that were harder to action.** Remember our friend who couldn't prepare her invoices, even when she tried to create an accounting habit? She overcame this problem by creating two keystone habits. 1) setting herself this rule: 'I will always do the hardest thing first' and 2) setting up a weekly meeting with a friend where they discussed their plans for the week, how they would action these plans and what they had achieved in the preceding week. If you are struggling with changing a specific behaviour, consider what keystone habit you could set up that would help your valued actions occur. For example, if you want to be more focused at work and better able to sleep at night, keystone habits proven to help are journaling, meditating and exercising in the morning. If this has got you interested in keystone habits, go through your list of hoped-for habits and circle the ones with a trickle-down effect and decide to start there.

7. **You fell foul of the 'what the hell effect'**, the experience that often occurs when we make one

bad decision, such as having the glass of wine we said we wouldn't have, and subsequently thinking "what the hell, I already broke my promise to myself, I may as well polish off the bottle now". The antidote to the 'what the hell effect' is 3-fold. Firstly, forgive yourself for slip ups and remind yourself everyone has them from time to time. Do this as shame and guilt only drives us to reach for more of whatever it is we said we would avoid, either as a way to soothe ourselves or to punish ourselves for our action. Secondly, remember that every single moment of your day is an opportunity to turn your habits around. If you slip up, whether it be in the morning, after lunch, or later on, it doesn't mean you have ruined it for the day and have to wait to start again tomorrow. You can choose to turn your habits around the moment you notice you are in the old habit. Thirdly, and this will be addressed properly later in the chapter, plan what you will do when you catch yourself in an old habit.

8. **You were self-sabotaging.** This will be fully addressed in Chapter 3.

Unsticking point

- Expect old habits to return. When stress or certain cues come knocking, habit loops you thought were a thing of the past may be reactivated. Whenever I work with someone who wants to change their habits, I say that the first step is learning to forgive yourself, as there are going to be points where you slip back into old ways. It is what you do next that matters. If you beat yourself up and see it as a sign that you will never make changes, you are unintentionally setting yourself up for that exact thing to happen. If, however, you forgive yourself and know this is part of the cycle of creating a lasting habit, you are on the path to success.

The best time for new habits

I have a confession to make. Whenever I read a new piece of research or hear about a psychological theory that has tips for how to overcome a specific challenge in life, I immediately put the ideas to the test. But, when I first started reading about the preparation required to change your habits, I resisted. I couldn't bring myself to do the work required to set up a schedule for my new habits. Underneath the resistance was a belief that I was a free spirit and having structure would surely take the spontaneity out of life. When I got curious about my free-spirited ways, however, I realized that my days were more chaotic than spontaneous.

My mornings involved falling out of my messy bed at the last possible moment into a big cup of coffee, doing a crossword while drinking said coffee, running to the train very late, and arriving at my first meeting after everyone else was sat down and introductions had been completed. The rest of my day would continue in the same vein. Even though my calendar would have been booked a week in advance, it seemed as if I was always on the back foot, surprised by what I had to do next. The only things I truly managed to get done were work- and deadline-related, and they were only completed so as not to put others out. Anything that was just for me, such as playing my Casio keyboard, meditating or going for a walk, went out the window as there was seemingly never any time to do it. I had to admit to myself that I was stuck, and something needed to change, so I delved back into the literature I had been avoiding and reacquainted myself with the following facts.

The easiest way to develop new habits is not to set a strict hourly schedule (e.g. 'I will drink water every hour', or 'at 12 p.m. every Sunday I will call my grandma'), but to use existing habits as cues for whatever you would like to add. This might be a case of making sure you finish the glass of water on your desk every time you stand up or calling your grandma when the final plate goes in the dishwasher on a Sunday. Stack your activities so that, with enough repetition, they become new, automatic behaviours with readily available cues. And, for bonus points, leverage your biological clock . . .

Did you know that in the first eight hours after waking, your brain chemistry is primed for you to take on your most challenging tasks? This is because you have the highest levels of norepinephrine, dopamine, cortisol and other chemicals that increase your alertness and focus. This is therefore the time to implement your most challenging new habits, as you are most likely to be able to face the resistance that often arises when you have to do something new or difficult.

In the second eight hours of the waking day, your brain chemistry changes: serotonin increases while those others I mentioned decrease, making you feel more relaxed. This is the time to schedule the activities that are already routine and/or the more soothing habits you want to engage in, such as mindfulness, yoga and journaling. And then in the final eight hours of the day, the period in which many of us (unless you are a shift worker or a new parent) are asleep, our brain consolidates the learnings of the day and rewires.

After learning this, I set up my own experiments. I knew I wanted to be in control of my day, so I completed the activities you have done so far in this chapter, and then made a plan of how and when I would do each activity. I wrote the following plan for each morning, both using the stacking-habits technique and the knowledge that we should try to do the most challenging things in the morning, which for me involves tidying the house!

When I wake up and get out of bed (the action I do every day that became the new cue), I immediately make my bed (this is the new response, which then becomes the cue for the next activity). Then I immediately moisturize my face and brush my teeth (something I always do but now becomes the cue for the next activity). Then I go downstairs and organize the sitting room (new routine, which becomes the cue for my old routine). I turn on the coffee machine, then I take my vitamins, which are next to the coffee machine (a bonus behaviour I added). When the light goes green, I then make coffee and drink it (reward). I do one crossword (reward), then I put my coffee mug in the sink and, as I walk past it, I play my keyboard for ten minutes (both a behaviour and a reward). Morning routine complete.

After writing this list, I moved my moisturizer out of the cupboard and put it next to my toothbrush, I put my vitamins next to the coffee machine and (rather more challenging) I moved my keyboard to a new position between the kitchen and my front door, so that seeing each item cued my new habits. After following this routine for a week, I realized that robotically cuing my behaviours and repeating them gave me a freedom I hadn't experienced before, and after a few weeks I was getting to the train on time with a clear head and a tidy house.

When trying to adopt new habits, consider whether you have any beliefs that will get in the way of you taking time to plan for the change you will need to make, and then consider which part of your day they'll fit into based on what energy level they will use. Once an activity is fully habitual, you will not need to be so strict about the timing, but this is a helpful guideline.

In case you are thinking, *Hang on, you just said don't start too many new habits at once, but now you're adding multiple habits to your morning routine,* you would be correct. However, I grouped them all into one seamless chain of events, and set up my environment in such a way that it was only one new routine, and nothing additional had to be held in mind.

Setting your new habits at times that work for your body

Return to Appendix 1 and the habits you are going to make part of your life. Complete column nine. Ask yourself: what portion of the day does each new habit fit best? The first eight hours? The afternoon? Then consult your daily timetable and the list of your habits. What habits do you already engage in around those times that you could attach your new habit to? Slot that new habit in directly after the habit you already have. Use the end of the previous activity to cue the new one.

Unsticking point

- You need to plan, plan and plan some more if you want to make real change. What are you going to do? When?

Help, I'm stuck

'I have a new lease of life now that my OCD feels under control and am trying to get into new activities, but honestly, after a great start, I think I may be getting worse at everything I am trying.'

—ZAC, 40

Zac had come to therapy to manage his intrusive thoughts – the kind that insert themselves into your day and terrify you into believing that you could be capable of doing something unthinkably awful, and that should you share that you had such terrifying thoughts with someone, they would have you locked up immediately as you were a danger to society. It took him eleven years from his first intrusive thought to contact a therapist, as he was so sure that this was a character flaw and not a mental health issue. The tears that ran down his face through the first sessions told of the pain he carried alone, the panic and sleepless nights he had endured, and the lengths he had gone to to suppress these thoughts, which he (incorrectly) thought must be impulses. He said he hoped I could help but he understood that I likely needed to call the police and that I was probably disgusted with him. As his head hung forward over his slumped shoulders, it felt more like a confession than a request for therapy.

The relief he experienced learning that the thoughts were just that – thoughts – and that there were not only many people who lived with the same experiences he had, but that exposure and response prevention was a very effective form of treatment for this, which we could start immediately, was only outshone by the day when he could confidently say that the intrusive thoughts were a thing of the not-too-distant past. His lust for life following this was a joy to behold. He had worked so hard in therapy, and now it was time to reap the rewards. He didn't want grand changes. He wanted a life that set him up for feeling good. This included regular exercise (he wanted to run), time for rest and play (he enjoyed the piano, learning Spanish and seeing his friends), and he wanted to write. I am sharing this story because I want to illustrate how much Zac wanted change. He was ravenous for a new life and was prepared to give it his all.

We worked on building his new habits into his life. We removed any friction that might stop him from engaging in his chosen habits (i.e. we removed cues that triggered old habits and inserted cues that made him more likely to do these activities), but after a few weeks he came back to me and told me he didn't want to do these activities anymore. The wind had gone from his sails. He was about to quit, as the tasks were seemingly getting harder not easier. He believed this meant that he was failing. Does this resonate?

When you start a new habit, you may, like Zac, manage to jog further than you imagined on your first few trips out or beat someone at tennis even though you have only played twice. You may pick up five new words in Spanish or grind out 1,000 words of a novel with ease. But then, following this, you may, like Zac did, notice you hit a plateau where no progress is observable. Running feels impossible, your tennis balls no longer get over the net, the Spanish vocabulary has disappeared, and your writing starts to feel as clear as mud.

The reality is that the natural process of learning involves the 'valley of disappointment', as James Clear so brilliantly calls it in *Atomic Habits*. Think about something you can do now that you were once terrible at. Are you able to speak a second language? Can you ride a bike? Can you cook a complex array of foods that you once couldn't even say the name of? Have you ever been able to walk? I ask about walking because if the answer is yes, this means you have fallen over and picked yourself back up thousands of times (on average, twelve- to nineteen-month-olds take 2,368 steps per hour and fall seventeen times in that sixty-minute period).[10] As babies we were all like the mouse I told you about earlier in the chapter, who managed to overpower even the strongest mice to get to the heat lamp, simply by repetitively trying over and over again.

As an adult, can you imagine failing at something seventeen times an hour and carrying on? This sounds horrifying, but the more mistakes we make, the faster we learn, as the mistake causes the brain to pay attention and leads to greater neural plasticity (readiness to make changes and create new neural pathways). But this can only happen if we do not panic about making mistakes. Remember when I said that the optimum difficulty of any new task or habit you start is something you can repeat accurately 85 per cent of the time? This means that when we are learning at our absolute best, we are still making mistakes 15 per cent of the time.

Zac didn't like to hear this, and neither did I when I was first studying habits. Few of us want to believe it, but the phrase 'it takes a lifetime to create an overnight success' is accurate. James Dyson, the inventor of the Dyson vacuum cleaner, 'burst' onto the scene following fifteen years of hard, unseen work making 5,127 prototypes before reaching the model that made him famous. Colonel Sanders, of KFC fame, had his chicken recipe rejected 1,000 times before hitting the right finger-licking ingredients in his fifties. If you've seen *Jurassic Park*, you will remember that the velociraptor tried every part of the park fence until it found the weak spot. They all plugged away, past the failures. You did it as a child to be able to do any of the things you consider habitual today, and you can do it again now.

Next time you start something, do what the author of *Hooked: How to Build Habit-Forming Products*, **Nir Eyal, says and** *aim to be an amateur.*[11]

Aiming for immediate success will make us miserable, as no one is truly spectacular at every task they turn their hand to. The difference between amateur and professional is that a professional can guarantee that (should no random variable arise) the outcome they intend will be achieved almost every time (e.g. their tennis shot will be guaranteed to land in the part of the court they want it to, or their finger will hit the note they aim for even when they are not looking at the piano keys). An amateur, on the other hand, is more likely to hit and miss at random, until the practice is consolidated.

Focus on the learning period, seeing the value of the moments you spend applying yourself to that activity, as the win, rather than on the outcome. When you notice thoughts such as *This is hard* or *I am rubbish at this*, reframe them in terms of being an amateur – *It feels hard because I am learning; it is normal; it will get easier with time; every time I get something slightly wrong my brain pays more attention, meaning I will learn faster.* I am not saying aim for mediocre. No. Babies don't learn to walk because they are okay with average; they give the period of learning their all. They practice straightening their legs, bobbing up and down at EVERY opportunity. They aren't giving up. They are pushing through.

Plan for the moments when you slip back into old habits

When trying to create a new habit, at some point it will get temporarily harder and old habits will likely sneak back in.

- **Repeat after me:** *Slipping back into an old habit or temporarily dropping a new habit is not a sign of failure. It is a common but uncomfortable part of habit change. When it happens, I will forgive myself. And I will start working on my habits afresh as soon as I am able to.*

- **Plan what you will do when you catch yourself in an old habit and write it in column ten of your table in Appendix 1.** For example, if you are trying to create focused working habits but find yourself scrolling on the phone, you could use this as a cue to hide your phone from view and turn back to the task at hand. Or, your replacement behaviour could be something totally different that addresses why you might be checking your phone in the first place. I now see checking my phone as a sign I am getting bored and immediately use it as a cue to stand up and stretch before returning back to the task at hand. If you notice you keep texting your ex during times of loneliness or sadness, you could use the moment you reach for the phone as a cue to practice the STOP technique, as this will not only help you get back in control of the moment, but also help you identify and soothe whatever emotional state cued you to reach for the phone in the first place. Or, you could use it as a cue to text a friend who will meet your needs instead. Whatever you choose, repeat this action every time you catch yourself slipping into bad habits. Over time this new behaviour will be associated with your old cues, and in the end the old habit will start to disappear as the new one kicks in.

- **Replace visualizing success with visualizing failure.** When we start a new activity, positive visualization can help motivate us to start. However, continuously visualizing success can drain our motivation, by triggering a relaxation response.[12] When you think about failure, your brain becomes alert, sensing a potential threat may be on the horizon, and a spike of fear or disappointment can usefully motivate you into action. Not only that, but it also gives you an opportunity to mentally overcome whatever failure scenario you envision. Important note: this is not the same as beating yourself up. Use positive imagery when you feel anxious and like you can't try, and negative when you need a kick up the bum. Not the other way round. Punishing yourself makes you much less likely to try as well. We are always trying to find the midline, which simply says 'try again' and gives you the energy to do this.

- **Think about that mouse making it under the heat lamp!** While writing this book there were so many moments where my new daily writing routine nearly fell apart during the learning phase of the habit. Writing a whole book involves such a huge period of writing utter crap that is boring and unreadable, which didn't make me feel good. Yet when I imagined that mouse, simply pushing and pushing over and over for that warm spot, I trusted that if I repeated the action of sitting down to write enough times, it would suddenly and one day be finished – and, well, you have the proof of that in your hands.

Unsticking point

- The habit is going to get harder to engage in before it gets better. Aim for average. Have a plan for managing the hard times.

Making change stick

The final barrier to change is one few people expect. Sometimes, the reason we can't change our behaviour is because we simply don't want to. I have seen this so many times in my career: the drinker who dabbles in sobriety courses, never quite committing to them; the person who goes to therapy to address their anger, who never puts any of the given strategies into practice; the serial monogamist who says they want an extended period of being totally single (no dating, just friendships), who swipes and chats to people on the apps each night; all of whom may not realize that they aren't deeply motivated to change yet. People tend to stay in this phase if they are what we call 'pre-contemplative' or 'contemplative'.

The transtheoretical model of change, which was devised by Prochaska and DiClemente in the 1970s, has seven stages, but for our purposes we only need to focus on the first two:

1. Precontemplation stage

In this stage, the cons list of changing our behaviour far out-weighs the pros – e.g. *Quitting X would . . . affect my social life/ make me less fun/take more time than I have/lead to stress, which isn't worth it right now as, seriously, how bad is it to do X every day anyway?!* We likely know that we are in this stage if pressure from others makes us defensive. The reality is, we won't move from this stage until we see the problem for ourselves. This is the stage I was at when I kept avoiding trialling out the habits research for myself. And this can be the stage the people in our life are at when we point out that they are repetitively doing something that seems to be harming them, but they don't appear to take it on board.

2. Contemplation stage

This is when we recognize our behaviour is a problem and intend to stop it. We may still be ambivalent, as we see there is an uphill struggle ahead, but we intend to make change within the next six months. We can stay in this stage for a while, aware of the issues but waiting for that final piece of information that will tip us over the edge.

If you think you are in either of these stages, remember: you get to choose what you do. Start paying attention to the actual impact of the habit you engage in. Don't just take other people's word that the behaviour is 'bad'. Get that mindfulness practice I mentioned earlier into your daily practice and start being seriously curious about how the action you are engaging in is impacting your life, health and relationships. This will not be a quick fix, but it will start you on your way. Then, think about who you could be if you changed this habit. Your best hope. Evaluate the difference between where you would like to be in life and where you are now. Identify the barriers that might be standing in the way of you taking positive action and decide how you will address them. If thoughts such as *It will be too hard* arise, recall something you did in the past that was difficult and that you succeeded at. Create 'I will . . .' statements around your intended new behaviour and visualize yourself having succeeded at that thing and living your life one year from now.

From here, you will then (hopefully) progress to the next four stages: Preparation (identifying which cues and obstacles need to be removed and what support needs to be introduced); Action (getting it done and giving yourself rewards);

Maintenance (focusing on repetition and noticing the fruits of your labour); Relapse (because we all end up here at some point; it's normal); Termination (when the desire to engage in the old habit is gone at last).

The termination phase sounds like a dream, doesn't it? Not to demoralize you, but for many of us, termination remains a dream, because most of us usually exist within the maintenance phase. Why? Because (trust me, I know from personal experience) things happen in life that shove us back down the old pathway. But that's okay, because every time we get back on our new path, we strengthen our belief that we can indeed choose a new way of life. That's all habits are, after all: doing the damn thing again and again.

Understanding how habits work is useful in understanding your own behaviour, but also that of the people around you. If you know someone who is repeating patterns that you think need to change, remember that everything in this chapter applies to them too. Use this knowledge to empathize with why they may do what they are doing, and why it may be obvious to you why they need to change but totally unclear to them. Remember that it is up to them to decide to change, but that you can also offer your perspective on how the actions impact your life and theirs. You can ask them to get curious about whether they agree with your observations, and about times in the past when they have made change in their lives that made them feel proud. You can, if they are up for it, identify the cues in the environment that are triggering old habits and remove them together. You could, in fact, give them this book and see what they do with the newly learned information, and let them decide for themselves whether they are ready to get unstuck.

Chapter 2

Heuristics

In 1961, President John F. Kennedy agreed to send 1,400 troops to invade Cuba and overthrow Fidel Castro. It was assumed the invasion would be a success, when in reality the Cuban air force and 20,000 Cuban fighters were ready and waiting for them. The attempted invasion was a catastrophic failure, and every one of the troops sent by America was either captured or killed.

A subsequent investigation into how the Bay of Pigs invasion became such a colossal disaster forced everyone, including the strategists who conceived of the plan to invade, to examine how they missed what they now saw were such obvious risks. The conclusion: during the planning stages, people were so determined to succeed that when a plan was offered, no one questioned it and they overlooked potential flaws. The plan had been devised by the previous president, Dwight D. Eisenhower, and the Central Intelligence Agency. When JFK came into office, he was brought in on the plan and signed off on it. The old and new presidents didn't challenge it, and the people who had reservations kept silent.

Irving Janis, a psychologist who analysed this disaster, said they likely experienced what he went on to call 'groupthink': the human tendency to share the most widely held opinion, to see the world through the eyes of the group, overlooking ideas and data that run contrary to the group's belief.

Determined to learn from their mistakes, JFK gave his brother, Attorney General Robert Kennedy, the role of official 'devil's advocate' during decision-making meetings. Devil's advocate was a role created not to be contrary or pick holes in ideas for the sake of it, but to ensure that 'groupthink' could no longer run the show. This person's job was to constantly offer a different perspective, slow down the process and ensure that decisions were made based on analysis rather than the excitement of the mob. It also helped address power dynamics in the group; I mean, even without groupthink, I wouldn't feel comfortable questioning the president and a room full of qualified people. Would you?

I am telling you this story as, although you and I may not be responsible for decisions that could kill thousands, this experience is something we could all learn from. Why? Because the second major reason we get stuck in our lives is that we often struggle to make decisions that are in our best interests. Not because we are stupid or because we lack access to the data or people who could guide us towards an accurate answer – as was clearly demonstrated in the example above – but because our decision-making is affected by many heuristics (we will learn more about these in a moment) and biases, such as groupthink, that can cause us to choose a particular course of action without even questioning whether it is the right thing to do.

This chapter will help you identify the heuristics and biases that influence how you see the world and the decisions you make. It will also show you when and where you, like JFK, need to take extra measures that will ensure you can think clearly and make important choices in your life that don't leave you feeling stuck.

What are heuristics?

Most of us believe that we make decisions using logic. We assume that we choose what we do, what we buy and who we listen to based on facts and data. However, as you have seen so far, this isn't always the case. Instead of making conscious decisions every time we face a dilemma, we often use shortcuts. These shortcuts – otherwise known as heuristics – reduce our mental effort, simplify hard questions and make us biased towards certain answers.

Some sources report that over 100 heuristics and (subsequent) biases exist, and chances are you're already familiar with a fair share of them. From the sunk-cost fallacy and groupthink to the halo effect and social proof – concepts we will discuss in detail in this chapter – heuristics and biases affect almost every decision we make. They help us solve our most trivial dilemmas and our biggest problems, fast. Most of the time, they are pretty accurate, but because they give us a best guess instead of a perfect answer, they aren't failproof.

If you need some convincing that heuristics and biases play a part in your life, consider the following questions. How often has your mood affected the decisions you make? Maybe a friend asked if you fancied a drink next Friday, but at the time she asked, you were having a bad day and you decided it didn't sound that appealing and wouldn't be worth the hassle. This is because of the 'affect heuristic' – the tendency to use your mood to guide your judgement of the situation you are in.

Maybe you've met someone you find attractive and automatically thought highly of them when you know nothing else about them. Or maybe you've done the opposite – writing someone off because of a stereotype you once heard that makes you think you know something about the person in front of you, when they haven't even had a chance to introduce themselves. No one likes to admit that these kinds of snap judgements occur, as we know they are usually inaccurate and biased, but nevertheless, they do happen. Why? Because of the 'halo effect': the tendency to make snap decisions about someone or something based on very little information. It's as if one feature acts as a halo (either positively or negatively) that shines over their entire persona, shaping our whole view of them.

Still not sure if heuristics and biases impact the decisions you make? Okay, how many times have you chosen the quick win over the choice that would support your future? Maybe you've decided to go for a fancy dinner over putting that same amount into a retirement fund. Or maybe you bought something on credit, rather than waiting until you had saved and could afford it at a later date. These instances are common because of 'hyperbolic discounting' – the tendency to prefer smaller rewards that are immediate, discounting the value of options that occur in the future, even when waiting would lead to a significant payoff.

No wonder so many of us feel stuck. We tend to choose things based on our mood (which for most people is about as reliable as the British weather), make snap judgements about the people, places and things in our lives based on very little information, and opt for the thing in front of us rather than remembering to play the long game. On top of all that, heuristics arise so quickly that we are rarely conscious of the fact that they are there at all.

Heuristics and biases can stop us from knowing what we want, what we believe and what we should choose. It isn't all doom and gloom, however – and there are good reasons that heuristics exist.

Why we have heuristics

Over the decades of work done in this field, there have been ongoing debates about why humans use heuristics to make decisions. Some researchers (notably Daniel Kahneman and Amos Tversky, the founding fathers of behavioural economics and the study of heuristics) believe heuristics exist because humans have limits to their cognitive capacity. We often use best guesses to save the time it takes to make difficult decisions. They say heuristics make us predictably irrational.

Others (notably the German psychologist Gerd Gigerenzer) believe heuristics provide helpful rules of thumb to get you to the best answer most of the time. So much so that medical professionals (and other life-protecting professions) actively use heuristics when decisions need to be made quickly. Instead of using complex machinery the instant a baby is born, the initial health is assessed with one question: *Is the baby crying?*

(If a baby is crying, it is likely to be healthy.) Likewise, the FAST acronym is used as an efficient way to get people who are having a stroke the required medical attention they need: is the face drooping? Can they lift both arms? Is their speech okay? If there are any deficiencies – facial droop, arm drift or speech slurring – it is time to get to a doctor.

Heuristics may be one of the ways we evolved to survive as a species.

The affect heuristic (using your emotion to judge the situation you are in) meant our ancestors acted according to gut instinct, which was instrumental when it came to being alert to danger.

Hyperbolic discounting (choosing the quick win over long-term gain) meant our ancestors would take opportunities as they presented themselves. If you see berries or a deer that could make a delicious meal tonight, you take them. You don't wait until the berries have become a bush, or until the deer has fattened up, as you might not be around then. Thinking about the future was pointless if you did not survive the now.

Groupthink (getting carried away by the ideas of others) may have supported social connections within the tribe, helping them get to a solution quickly. Whether that solution was brilliant or a Bay-of-Pigs-level disaster, groups (even when affected by groupthink) outperform informed individuals once a task gets complicated.[1]

Even the halo effect might have been useful. Did you know humans are thought to have outlived other hominid species by befriending and working together with 'in-group strangers' (i.e. strangers who shared similar – *Homo sapiens* – characteristics to them at that time)?[2] It is possible that the halo effect helped us identify shared characteristics and bring those people in.

Whether you believe heuristics are rational or not, what is clear is that these systems of thinking worked well in the relatively simple environment we evolved in. And they still work well in high-risk and/or time-limited situations. In the modern world, however, decisions are generally more complicated and less dangerous. We don't need the quick fix or to make the decisions our ancestors made to survive, and we certainly don't want to be making snap judgements about people based on single characteristics. Instead, we need to be able to recognize and override heuristics or make them work for us.

Unsticking points

- We can get stuck in our lives because we are programmed to use rules of thumb to make decisions that will give us a best guess, not the best answer.
- People assume that, should they wish to change their lives, they simply need to focus on their daily actions. The reality is, being human is far more complex than that and many of our 'bad habits' aren't simply the physical actions we engage in each day; some of them play out in our heads and our judgements.

Help, I'm stuck

'I lost a close friend recently, and ever since she died I am more aware than ever that life is short, but I have no idea what to do with the time I have on this planet. I was

thinking about moving out of the countryside and into the city, but maybe that's not a good decision. All my friends are doing it, but is it for me? I follow chefs who chase down amazing experiences, and interior designers who post beautiful beach pictures and say following their dreams has brought them so much happiness. Would quitting my job and travelling stop me from feeling stuck? I don't want to be a sheep, but I want to do something. Not only am I stuck choosing what to do next, I realize I have rarely made my own choice in life and stuck to it. People keep saying carpe diem, but I can't carpe anything if I don't know what I want in life, can I! What should I do?'

—ALESSIA, a client of mine

Alessia came to therapy at the age of fifty-two following the death of a beloved friend. She was the kind of friend that was more like a sister, or platonic life partner, that you would discuss everything and nothing with at any time of day. They prided themselves on being 'in the know' about the location of the next hot-ticket event, what was in the news and in the zeitgeist. But they were silly together too. The day her friend died, Alessia's world as she knew it had been taken from her.

Through discussing her grief, she had come to the conclusion that she needed to find a way to mourn the loss but also find a way to continue living. We interwove discussions of her friend and their times together with periods of silence, when the waves of pain would eclipse her ability for speech, and with periods of getting to know Alessia as a person – what she liked, disliked, who she was, who she had been and who she would be moving forward. When we first ventured into discussing her future life, she would say a few words and instantly stop. She would say it felt shallow. Not simply because it felt so trivial a discussion when compared to the death of her friend, but because when she heard herself speak out loud about what she might do next, discussing the Instagram posts and the beaches, she sounded 'inane', like the kind of person she and her friend would secretly roll their eyes at on the bus and then giggle about openly once the doors had closed firmly behind. At this point she would smile, reliving the memory, and then she would cringe – 'Maybe we were judgemental too.'

Alessia was not alone in thinking that taking time to dream about a future isn't a 'serious' person's pastime. I see it often, and it usually goes hand in hand with believing that being optimistic is a fool's errand. But questioning what you do with your time is not inane; it matters. As does having hope. As you already know, one of the many reasons we get stuck in life is because we don't pause and ask, *What am I doing right now?* and *What will I do next?* often enough. It took some time for Alessia to feel convinced of this, but as the grief lifted enough for her to consider a future, she decided to live the kind of life that her friend would be proud of. She told me she would be back next week with a plan ... But by the time of her next appointment, she realized she was stuck.

Until that point, Alessia had made most of her life choices based on what her friends had suggested. Making decisions for herself had her at a loss.

Like so many people I meet, she felt stuck and without direction. She knew she wanted to make a change in her life that suited her, but what kind of change?

Unlike JFK, Alessia didn't have a room full of world experts to guide her, but she was aware of groupthink and was determined to overcome it. To try to mitigate it, she looked outside of her immediate circle, casting her net further afield to people on social media and in the news who could offer her some unexpected options for moving forward. Unfortunately, the more she looked, the more overwhelmed she became.

Can you think of a time when you haven't known what decision would be best for you? It could have been something as small as wondering which hobby or exercise class to take up next, or it could be something as life-changing as wondering whether to leave a partner or a job. Did you notice that even though you wanted to make a decision that was based on your own opinions, it was hard to, due to the pull of other people's thoughts and behaviours? If you answered yes, it isn't solely because of groupthink. We are also affected by 'social proof' – the tendency to look at what other people do in any situation and copy it.

Social proof is compounded if the person we look to has a big social media following. Do you remember when the actress and business mogul Gwyneth Paltrow suggested we steam-clean our vaginas, an action which led one woman to suffer second-degree burns and need reconstructive surgery?[3] People ignored the warnings and the fact that Gwyneth was not a health professional, and within days there was a spate of Instagram pictures of people, you guessed it, perching over the steam. Or, do you remember when Donald Trump was the President of the United States of America and said people should ingest bleach to overcome Covid-19? Disinfectant poisoning in the next eight days rose by 121 per cent.[4] People engaged in these extremely dangerous behaviours in part because of social proof – the belief that the opinions of high-profile people, irrespective of their credentials, must be correct because so many people follow them.

Alessia had tried to look outside of her group but fell into the trap of social proof elsewhere. The belief that people with status must be good and/or right and we should listen to their ideas and copy their behaviours is why Alessia was so compelled by the stories of those she followed online. It wasn't just the blue sky or a yearning for sunshine; it was also the 'verified' blue tick next to an influencer's name that suggested she was someone to listen to. *If she says this is what I should do, then she must be right!*

Around 2.8 billion people use Facebook, 2.3 billion people use YouTube and 1.8 billion people use Instagram, many of whom, whether qualified to give advice or not, share their top tips on living a good life every day ... 'Get married; the research says it will make you happier'; 'Fuck marriage; research says it's likely to end in divorce'; 'Buy a house and get on the housing ladder'; 'Live in a van; don't do what society says you should do!'; 'Be sexy, get ripped, be the best you can be'; 'You are enough as you are'. No wonder Alessia was unsure what she wanted. We live in a time in which our decision-making skills have never been more challenged.

Most of us want to avoid having regrets. We know we want to live a life true to ourselves. We know we don't want to be sheep, but we don't realize we are programmed to follow the flock. Also, few of us know how to identify what we truly want. Well, not anymore. For Alessia and those of you wanting to get unstuck, the first thing to do is to get to know what heuristics and biases are, why and when they occur, and how to sidestep them when necessary.

Unsticking point

- When our heuristics run unchecked, we tend to make decisions that maintain the status quo, fit with the group, or ignore beliefs that don't align with ours.

System 1 vs system 2 thinking

When Daniel Kahneman and Amos Tversky put forward the idea of heuristics, they also proposed two systems of thinking that could explain how and when heuristics were used.

System 1 is automatic, emotional, and ancient. It's the system that's used when you repeat an old habit. This system is so effective at repeating your habitual actions that it works better when you aren't actively concentrating on what you are doing. Have you ever overthought your breathing and suddenly felt like you weren't quite getting enough oxygen, as it didn't seem like you were inhaling right? Or repeated a word multiple times and thought, *Hang on – it seems weird*.

This system is full of heuristics. You are using it whenever you have a gut feeling about something. For example, it will prompt you to walk out of the bar that feels sketchy, or lead firefighters to tell their team to get out of a building because something doesn't feel right when nothing is visibly wrong.

System 1 decision-making – i.e. how most of our unconscious decisions are made

Situation (a moment where a decision is made)

↓

Heuristic (rule of thumb or subsequent bias arises instantaneously, guiding our thinking)

↓

Decision (arises like a flash)

System 2, on the other hand, is slow, deliberate, and calculating. It helps you do more complex tasks that you have to slow down for, such as calculating who owes what when splitting a bill in a restaurant with friends, working out how much extra food to buy for dinner when an unexpected guest says they'd love to come over, and when writing an email to explain something complicated to a colleague. These conscious and unconscious systems of thinking interact all the time. If you are a habitual worrier whose self-criticism pops up repeatedly – *Oh my god, I am going to bomb this interview* – it is system 2 that (hopefully) steps in with *That is unlikely, you haven't failed before, and even if you do fail, it won't be the end of the world*. When you put this book down and start practicing overcoming the heuristics that keep you stuck, it will be system 2 that you need to engage, as it will help you override the pull of the thoughts of others and the biases that sneak into your everyday judgements.

Getting to know how heuristics affect you

1. Think about the big decisions you have made in life. How did you make those decisions? List some of the biggest decisions you have made (e.g. dating/not dating someone; starting up/not starting a business). List how you made those decisions. Did you look up the odds of succeeding? Did you go based on your gut? If the latter, which heuristic do you think you were using? (E.g. did the halo effect make you jump into something with a hottie, whose looks made you disbelieve others' comments that you should steer clear? Did groupthink within a community of nervous nellies put you off starting a business that you truly believed would work?) Did your decision work out for you?

2. **Using the STOP technique from Chapter 1 (page 22), spend the next twenty-four hours paying attention to the moments where snap judgements arise.** Get curious about the heuristics and biases you may be using. For example, you may notice that when someone asks you, 'How did your interview go?', you instead answer the question: 'How did you feel during the interview?' as the affect heuristic pops up again. Once you notice a snap judgement or bias, consider what might be missing from your thinking. For example, if the

affect heuristic really is the issue, remember feelings are not facts and aim to separate the two. *I feel
like it didn't go very well as I have a tendency to assume
I will fail everything I try. The reality is I did my best,
answered all the questions, but found one of them so hard
I almost didn't answer it at all.*

Unsticking points

- Mindfulness is key to bringing system 2 online. It can
  help you slow down decision-making, allow emotions
  that affect your judgement to pass, and give you the
  awareness to notice which heuristic might be guiding
  your thinking. From there, you can then decide how
  to proceed.
- Everyone uses heuristics. Knowing about them can
  help you not only understand yourself but also understand the actions of those around you.

When should you go with your gut?

'Just trust your gut' is a common expression that I tussle with
often. It is true that sometimes our gut instinct is correct,
but this statement overlooks the complexity of decision-
making. And, for people who live with anxiety, OCD, or
who have experienced trauma, trusting your gut can feel

impossible, as your gut sends mixed signals, often signalling danger when you are physically safe. So, when *should* you go with your gut?

It's generally okay to go with your gut when:

1. you don't have time to work out an accurate answer to the problem you are trying to solve
2. the outcome of your decision is based on luck
3. you don't have reliable statistics to shape your decision
4. you do not have a way to manage the stats should you have them to hand (either because they are too numerous or complicated)
5. you are extremely experienced in the area you are working in

The rest of the time we can make better decisions by taking our time, generating as many solutions as possible to the problem at hand, weighing up the pros and cons of each choice, and then picking one option to try initially, knowing you can choose another option from the list should that not work out (Appendix 2 has a premade problem-solving table you can use to practice this).

To really elevate our decision-making, we can look to the existing data available on our specific predicament. This latter point is tricky, as we exist in a time where people distrust data and statistics, as they can often seem confusing – conflicting, even – and because there are further heuristics that get in the way of us seeking and believing statistical data even when it does exist.

Help, I'm stuck

> *'Oh my god what do I do? I have my Covid-19 vaccine*
> *this afternoon, but I'm panicking. I cancelled the last three*
> *appointments because I'm so convinced something bad will*
> *happen. Most of my friends have their vaccines. They*
> *didn't worry about it at all. But every time I get near to*
> *an appointment the panic escalates to a fever pitch and*
> *all I can think of are the risks . . . What if I have the jab*
> *and then have a stroke or die? Oh god! I am going to call*
> *and cancel.'*

—ROSE

Rose showed up to our Wednesday morning session frantic. The moment the Zoom call connected, she jumped, dropping everything she was holding. She said she was 'a flustered mess', her thoughts and emotions as scattered as the contents of her bag that had recently hit the floor. I had known Rose for a year. She had been travelling at the start of the first Covid-19 lockdowns and, having missed the final flight back to the UK, she was one of the people the newspapers had reported were requesting the government find them a way home – unfortunately to no avail. The first few months had been okay, but then the realization that she was so far away from the people she loved, whom she worried about every day, started to take its toll. She began therapy to manage the loneliness and existential struggles that came with being stuck away from home during a global pandemic, and she had stayed in therapy after the struggles had passed as she wanted to unpick some relationship patterns that she now realized were an issue. We had met weekly for forty-five weeks and this was the first time she had mentioned her fears about the vaccine and the multiple cancellations. I was, therefore, surprised.

It transpired that, after cancelling her first vaccine appointment around nine months ago, Rose decided to ask a question about the safety of the vaccine on a well-known influencer's Instagram page, determined to learn more. She was immediately pounced on by people in the comments calling her 'anti-vaxxer scum', telling her she was 'everything that is wrong with this world'. People even went to her personal page to continue this rant. Following this, Rose shied away from asking people anything about the vaccine, and from telling anyone about her fears. Hence it taking until her fourth vaccine appointment to bring this up in therapy, as she knew that I was pro-vaccine and therefore thought this meant I might pounce on her too.

When we investigated Rose's fear, it turns out she wasn't an anti-vaxxer, or someone with a needle phobia or a pre-existing health condition that might explain the levels of panic she experienced, so what was going on? She was struggling due to 'the availability heuristic' – the tendency to make decisions based on the information that comes to mind the most easily, rather than based on data.

The newspapers in the country where Rose stayed during the first year of the pandemic reportedly focused less on the deaths from Covid-19 and more on the deaths from the vaccine. The information available to her told her that the vaccine was more dangerous than the virus. And the more she worried about what she read, the more readily available that worrying information became, compounding her fears. Have you ever noticed that happen before? Maybe someone you know died of a brain tumour, and every time you had a headache after this, you assumed it was cancer, as this was the information available to you about headaches. Maybe you noticed that the more you worried about it, the harder it became to shake the certainty that this was the cause of the pain. But, maybe, you also noticed that over time, when the worry subsided, you rarely assumed a headache was caused by this. This is what happens with the availability heuristic.

Rose was also affected by our old frenemy groupthink, which is having its moment in the sun on social media. Groupthink at its worst compels people to silence and/or to punish anyone who appears to have a different view to the group, even when they are not 'dissenting' but, like Rose, are simply being curious about the topic. No wonder Rose was stuck. She needed a place to understand the data, her fears, and talk it through, but had been bullied instead.

In terms of how we interpret data, there are other heuristics that affect us too. Take my family friend Bob, for example. Bob didn't want his child to get the vaccine, but not because he was anti-vaccine. When we chatted, he said, 'We were told that Covid-19 was safe for that age group, and now they say we need to get them vaccinated. I don't understand. It seems a bit shady.' People thought he was a conspiracy theorist due to the 'shady' remark, but he was simply affected by 'the anchoring effect' – the tendency to make decisions based on a reference point, usually the first piece of information we hear, even when subsequent information should change the way we think.

Rose and Bob had concerns and questions they needed to have answered. Heuristics caused them to ignore or distrust the data that was available to them, and worse than that, because of groupthink, they were shamed any time they asked important questions that could help them reach an informed decision. Once they had time to understand heuristics and biases, look through the actual statistics, and ask all their questions, they both felt much more comfortable to attend their vaccine appointments, holding a more balanced view of the risks in mind.

These heuristics affect each of us all day, every day, not just when it comes to making health-related choices. They change the way we make our decisions, based on the information we see first or most frequently and find the easiest to remember. This is a pressing issue, because we live in a world where the media thrives by selling one-sided and often inaccurate stories. Turn on the TV, look at social media, walk into your local newsagent, and whatever story is being peddled most vigorously is likely to become what anchors us.

Marketing and advertising also use heuristics against us. In 1929, Edward Louis Bernays, considered the founding father of public relations, popularized smoking – a traditionally male habit – for women by paying 'good-looking' women to march in the Easter Sunday Parade in New York, smoking their 'torches of freedom'. Pictures were published around the world, without mention of Bernays or the tobacco industry who had invested in his talents, meaning few realized this was a publicity stunt. Social proof and the halo effect meant women started to see smoking as a habit of the 'liberated woman', i.e. a very good thing. This kind of sales tactic has been used ever since. Nowadays you will hear upbeat music in the background of adverts so that our mood is lifted, and the affect heuristic makes us think, *Ooh, this brand must be good*, or there will be adverts with green backgrounds so that the halo effect tricks us into thinking the product is good for the environment and stops us from bothering to find out if this is true. You will come across companies that create in-groups and out-groups, so that if you buy their items you feel like you are better than the people who buy from other brands – if this sounds vague, consider the use of iPhones vs Androids, or MacBook vs PC and how so many of us identify ourselves depending on which of these we use. And while cigarette companies may no longer be able to sell their wares the way they used to, the practices employed back then are still very much in use. Consider the way advertisers dress their models up to look eternally young, rich and successful, so that we believe that those who buy this brand are 'better' people. And then, when they have us wanting what they are selling, they anchor us at one (potentially inflated) price point, and then slash costs to a lower one that we now think of as a bargain, even though the new cost may be more than we were originally planning to spend.

Every advert you see has been curated to ensure you want to reach into your pocket and pay for what they are selling – either by repeatedly showing you a brand so that you think of it first when you need to buy that item, or, more concerningly, by shifting the way you see the world, yourself and who is better or worse off.

So, keep your wits about you and drop your own anchor from time to time. For example, if you get offered a job and you are asked to state the amount you wish to be paid, you are more likely to secure a higher salary if you start the bidding and aim high, as once your future employer suggests a figure, that will be the anchor and everything will be negotiated from there.

The availability and anchoring heuristics underpin many other biases and behaviours. For example, the availability heuristic causes the halo effect, as stereotypes tend to be the first thing that come to mind when judging people we do not know. As for the anchoring heuristic, it underpins:

1. **The planning fallacy** – the tendency to underestimate how long it will take to do something even though you have done it before, and it took you ages to do. How many times have you been given a month to do a project and thought, *It will only take me a few days; I don't need to start now,* only to find you had to ask for an extension as it took longer than expected? The task suddenly seems harder than you thought it was, as you were anchored at, *It should only have taken a few days!*

2. **The spotlight fallacy** – the tendency to believe others are paying more attention than they really are to your actions. This arises because we are anchored to our own personal viewpoint, either in a positive way (when we assume others must be so impressed by our behaviour) or in the negative way (when we assume we are being judged harshly for every action). In reality, however, most people are so consumed with thoughts about themselves and

how they come across that they have little space left to think about you in this way!

Looking for statistics to guide decisions

1. **Think about a time when you made a decision.** Did you look up the stats or at your personal experience of doing this activity in the past? If so, did you pay attention to them? If yes, why? If no, why not?

   Did you get married without looking up the likelihood of divorce? Did you start smoking while ignoring the rates of cancer linked to it? If you answered yes to any of these questions, why do you think you overlooked the statistics? Is it because you didn't know the stats? Or didn't think to look? Was it that you were in a great mood at the time, and therefore the risks didn't feel so high and certainly didn't outweigh the advantages of saying 'yes' in the moment (another example of the affect heuristic)? Or was it because the availability heuristic was telling you neither of these activities were risky, as thinking of marriage brought to mind pictures of an elderly couple holding hands who have been together for life, or because smoking brought up the image of the 108-year-old, cigarette in mouth, saying she thinks smoking made her life better? Or was it because you knew

---

the stats and calmly thought, *I am willing to take the risk*? There is no specific lesson here; I just want you to get curious about these experiences.

2. **Think about an issue you are struggling with deciding over.** It could be to do with a vaccine, changing jobs, moving to a new city, or anything that you are wondering about right now. Are there any statistics or pieces of information that will help you decide?

Unsticking point

- When making important decisions, statistics and other available data can help, so look for the information you might be missing, and consider what heuristics may be at play.

Biases

How are you doing? Are you nodding along as you read about heuristics you now recognize but never realized were affecting you? Are you noticing that sometimes you may feel stuck as you struggle to drown out the opinions of others, or to see beyond your own knee-jerk reactions? Or are you seeing these examples as issues that happen to other people rather than yourself? I ask this question because one of the main barriers to overcoming heuristics is a blissful lack of awareness that we are affected by them at all. I know this as I have experienced it personally. I initially thought that the reason I found it so easy to believe others fell into these traps, and not me, was because I was too nervous to admit my own fallibility. My job involves listening to other people's experiences and struggles; it involves paying attention to where they get caught up in life, and answering their questions, meaning much of the time my focus is on the people around me and not myself. It turned out, it wasn't either of those things. It was because we (unsurprisingly) have more heuristics that blind us to our ignorance, including, but not limited to, confirmation bias and the illusory superiority heuristic.

1. Confirmation bias – paying attention only to evidence that reinforces pre-existing beliefs

There are so many examples of confirmation bias playing out in our lives. Maybe you only consume stories that show your political party is *good* while the other is *bad*. Maybe after a fight with your partner you only notice the aspects of their behaviour that prove they didn't listen to a word you said. Or maybe you interpret the actions of others as confirming your worst fears – e.g. if you think you are unlovable/ugly/stupid – and you start interpreting every action of the people in your life as confirmation of this.

Look, sometimes confirmation of our thoughts and feelings is not simply due to bias. Politicians will sometimes do something terrible, your partner may sometimes be insensitive, and it's a fact that sometimes we do stupid things that others will judge us for. But we must be careful, as confirmation bias means we ignore the information that would give us a true picture. We stay stuck as our brain is determined only to look for the information that proves where we are and what we believe to be true already.

And it isn't only our brains we need to watch out for. We are facing an onslaught of information designed to play on our propensity for confirmation bias. The algorithms on our smartphones pay attention to the information we look at and then deliver more and more of the same information to us so that we have fewer and fewer opportunities to check our facts. This allows disinformation to spread incredibly quickly. This can be because of something seemingly innocent, such as the number of characters allowed in a social media post, meaning nuanced information often gets lost, and with it the facts. Or because social media sites do not fact-check the opinions shared on their pages. Or because of something more malicious, such as organized disinformation campaigns. A terrifying example of the latter arose in the run-up to the 2016 American presidential election, where the Internet Research Agency, sponsored by the Kremlin, reportedly created over 3,500 adverts that fed fake news to specific social media users to harm the campaign of Hillary Clinton and swing the election in favour of Donald Trump.[5] Some 3.7 million users saw these adverts, which ranged between showing anti-immigrant information to people who followed personalities from the notoriously conservative American news outlet Fox News, to an advert that read, 'stop Islamophobia and the fear of Muslims' from an account called 'United Muslims of America', which looked to be real but was not, that was followed up with an open letter that accused Hillary Clinton of failing to support Muslims before the elections.[6]

It is important that we identify where heuristics arise in our daily life, and also when the greater powers in society tap into those heuristics and manipulate them, keeping us stuck. We could all benefit from playing devil's advocate to ourselves when we are certain about something we think is true. This is also why many people I know will now make a point of reading a news article a day (minimum) from the papers that directly oppose their views. They recognize that somewhere in the middle of each strong opinion is likely the truth. What will you choose to do to step outside your comfortable confirmation bubble?

If you read this and think, *Not me; I am not affected by that bias*, maybe you are right. People who have tried these exercises before and already know about how to manage heuristics are less likely to be caught out by biases; this is where I hope you will be by the end of the chapter. However, maybe you will be like me – yes, I am outing myself so you know there is no shame if this is you – and believe you are not affected by heuristics as we simply fall prey to another bias . . .

2. The illusory superiority heuristic – the tendency for people to overestimate their abilities

Did you know that 90 per cent of drivers believe they are better than average?[7] Or that 81 per cent of people believe they have a better than average chance of their business succeeding, even after being told that 50 per cent of new businesses fail?[8]

These statistical impossibilities are prime examples of illusory superiority.

This isn't a phenomenon that happens to 'other people'; it will happen to us all at some point, so we must keep an eye out for it. My own tussles with illusory superiority range from the trivial to the professional, but all hit me hard. For example, I thought I had a natural talent for drawing, having doodled a lot at home, and then went to a life-drawing class and met serious artists whose talent knocked my socks off and showed me my good command of stick men in no way qualified as real talent. When I had just completed a masters in neuroscience, I believed I had a comprehensive understanding of people and how they worked, and then met my first ever client in a mental health service, and immediately realized that people are far more complex than their biology, and will always surprise you. Illusory superiority rarely arises because we are arrogant or smug, although I definitely bordered on each of those presentations in the moments I just described. It usually happens because we simply aren't exposed to the full extent of a situation, i.e. how good the best drivers really are, or, in my case, what someone who really practices their art can achieve, or how complex human beings can be and what the human soul can survive. This means once we feel accomplished at something, we tend to assume we must be above average at that thing too.

Illusory superiority can be useful, as it leads to optimism and increased risk-taking in terms of business or other areas of life, rather than depressive realism, which can be associated with low mood and a belief there is no point in trying. Have you ever met someone new, been to a job interview – or even simply left your house in the morning – with a smile on your face, a sense that you can and will achieve whatever it is that you set out to do today, and noticed that other people respond positively to this? Returning your smile. Riffing off your comments. Asking if they can see you again, give you a job, or even their seat on the train? Then left the house the next day, not feeling quite so chipper, and found that the outcome of your day seemingly followed your mood, i.e. was a little flat too? If so, you know how radically our mindset can affect the outcome of the situation we are in. Don't automatically assume that illusory superiority is something to be avoided at all costs; in some situations, it may make you perform better simply because you feel more confident about the task at hand. However, overconfidence leading to increased risk-taking behaviour can be potentially deadly if this means speeding on the motorway, thinking your skill will protect you. People who have an inflated sense of ability are statistically more likely to cause accidents and make poor decisions in life (e.g. around money) and have even been blamed for wars,[9] and stock-market bubbles and crashes.[10]

And for some people who have a consistently inflated self-belief, another cause of 'stuckness' can arise in the form of anger that threatens to take over when failure or criticism comes their way. I had a client who would feel personally attacked when he failed or when his beliefs were challenged. He didn't realize that he was actually terrified that people would see him as flawed or unacceptable, or that the pumped-up version of himself that he often showed the world was actually a defence. For him, learning to recognize times where he overestimated his abilities, and that he was okay and normal to be someone who made mistakes, was scary, but also caused his anger to ebb. Over time he learned that people tended to prefer the humbler person he had become, which helped him continue down the path of being the imperfectly real version of himself.

On the other hand, some people experience worse-than-average bias, and that can arise due to low self-esteem and/or the way you were socialized. For anyone worrying about their self-esteem, I'll go into more detail about that in Chapter 3.

Understanding others

Everyone is affected by heuristics, so it is important to use your understanding of heuristics to try to understand others too.

Exercise: spend the next twenty-four hours considering what heuristics the people you meet may be using. Is your friend always late to meet you because they don't take your time seriously or is it because of planning fallacy, which makes them think the journey time will be significantly shorter than it is? Did your partner say, 'You never do ... [insert activity here]' because you never do it or because confirmation bias only allowed them to see what they fear may be true? Did your manager ignore a really important piece of new research that is integral to your work, as it doesn't confirm what he believes? Notice how you feel when

---

you do this. Does recognizing that there may be a heuristic causing their behaviour change how you feel about their decisions? Does it give you any ideas on how you could address the situations at hand? Instead of complaining about your friend's continual disrespect for timings, might you now want to point out the journey time to your friend? Instead of fighting with your partner, might you want to ask them if they can think of a time when you surprised them by doing the things they say you never do? Instead of agreeing with your manager, might you want to educate them in confirmation bias?

Unsticking points

- If you want to make better decisions, get comfortable with the idea that you might be missing something and may simply be wrong. Ask yourself these questions often: what data might I be missing? Am I gathering information from one source? Does my judgement/ feeling/decision confirm an old belief of mine, or does it challenge me? How often are my ideas questioned? How do I feel when questioned? How many of my friends have different views to me? What biases may I have internalized? What am I prepared to do about these answers?
- When making big decisions, imagine that you have to

explain your behaviour and beliefs to a jury. While this won't change the emotional state you are in when you make a decision, it will help you see the snap judgements and loopholes in your thoughts.

• Remember that everyone is affected by heuristics and knowing about this will help you understand yourself and also the actions of others.

What do you want?

Remember Alessia, whom we met at the beginning of the chapter? After we explored everything that you have just learned, she left that session excited about her new-found knowledge of heuristics. But she returned to the next session disgruntled. While it was a relief to know that certain biases were clouding her judgement, she said that I'd sent her off with the skills to drown out the factors that compete for her attention, but I hadn't taught her anything about how to figure out what she actually thinks. She was right. While the first step to making good decisions is becoming aware of the things that make us make bad choices, the second step is finding out what you truly believe. To answer this question, we need to know what we truly value in life.

What do you care about? What do you value in others? How would you like to be remembered? Have you taken the time to ask yourself these questions? Or do you tend to focus on goals over values? If you aren't sure what I mean, goals are the actions you can tick off a list – the pay rise, the partner, the house, the marathon – whereas values are the qualities that are important to you – freedom, compassion, stability, reliability, mastery, fitness. Goals are great in that they give us a point of focus and something to strive for, but even if we do achieve them, the ensuing happiness tends to be fleeting and then forgotten about as we move on to the next best thing. Values, on the other hand, act as a north star for us to chart the course of our lives by. Have you worked out your values before? If not, it's time to do it.

Getting to know what you truly want in life

1. **Number the following areas of life in order of importance to you.** Don't number them based on how much space they take up in your life right now. Consider instead what you truly care about and how, should you be able to create a life that you truly want, each of these valued areas would contribute to being that person (e.g. right now your career may take up all of your time, yet when you consider what you truly value, community, family and health may come first).

   ____ Health and physical wellbeing
   ____ Education and personal growth or development
   ____ Career
   ____ Recreation, leisure and fun times
   ____ Community involvement
   ____ Spirituality

_____ Friendships and social life
_____ Intimate relationships
_____ Parenting
_____ Wider family relationships

2. Starting with whichever area you rated as most important and moving down the list from there to the least important, write down what you value about that aspect of your life. For example, you may value your work as it gives you something to be passionate about, a place where you get to take responsibility and gain recognition for your efforts and affords financial security. In which case, your values linked to career would be passion, responsibility, feeling useful and security. Or you may value your personal time, because you learn new creative endeavours during these moments – in which case, your values linked to recreation may be creativity and mastery.

3. Write down how you would like to feel in each of these areas of your life, starting with the area that is most important to you. How you would like to feel are values, too. For example, in your intimate relationships you may value feeling connected to other people – in which case, your values would be connection, fun, collaboration and support.

4. Write down how you would like to be remembered by people when they discuss you after you have passed. Do you want to be remembered as hardworking? Reliable? Compassionate? We are looking for qualities, not tick lists. Add these qualities to your list of values.

5. Visualize where you would like to see yourself in six months, one year, five years and ten years. Ask yourself what qualities your future self has at each life stage. How do they identify? Are they healthy? Religious? Hard-working? Write down what values and goals this person has.

6. Look at the discrepancy between your values and how you are living today. Write down what you need to do to ensure you include more of your values in your day, and choose activities and goals that will lead you to become your desired future self. If you can't meet a goal because something unexpected has happened, i.e. you have an illness that means you cant run the marathon or need to take time off work, use the values that are linked to each of your goals to choose another activity that could meet those needs.

7. Return to the list of habits you created while reading the previous chapter and add any habits you think would help you to live a valued life and cross out any that go against your values.

Add the new habits to Column 6 in Appendix 1 and complete Columns 7-11 to plan how you will action these activities. Remember, however, to focus on one new habit at a time, or to choose a keystone habit that will influence all the activities you want to engage in, so you don't end up overloading your day with new activities.

8. Use the problem-solving exercise in Appendix 2 if you are not sure what actions you should take now that you know what you value. The question you are trying to solve depends on what you are wanting to do next, e.g. 'What should I do next with work?'

The final barrier

You nearly have all the information you need to get out there and get thinking clearly. But before I let you go and have a break before we hit Chapter 3, there is a final barrier and final person I want to tell you about. His story is one that affects most of us when people get to the point in their learning that we are now at.

Help, I'm stuck

'I've been in my job for five years. I love the job itself – I get to design and build things – and the first few years were

great. It was a small team so we could make choices on our own, we got paid well and were promised equity, but then the company grew rapidly. Now we don't get as much client contact, the equity never came through and we are more like cogs in a machine. The new boss treats everyone, particularly me, so badly. My partner has long commented that I don't seem happy, and I tell him I am going to leave every six months, but then something happens, and, well, I don't. At first my partner got angry at the business on my behalf as he knows how hard I work, but now he seems to be getting mad at me as I don't leave. What do I do? I am pretty sure I want out and I know what I would do instead but I can't seem to make the leap.'

—JAMAL, 29

Jamal came to therapy as he was in a long-term committed relationship with a man he loved deeply who he was about to move in with. And, while to many this sounded like a dream come true, it was giving him nightmares. He had a history of depression and a partner had left him when he was at a very low ebb a few years ago, stating he was 'too hard to be with'. What if his new partner moved in and then thought the same? To tackle this, we not only worked on relapse prevention for his mood, but we also focused on learning how to identify which of his thoughts were anxiety and which indicated a concrete issue that needed tackling. The quote above is a snapshot of one of the many things that were triggering his fears. The situation stood out as it was the first example Jamal brought to therapy that his partner had actively suggested he

share with me. Jamal was terrified that his partner's suggestion was proof that he thought he was mad and would leave.
We did our usual activity of putting the thought on trial,
looking for the evidence for and against this thought. And
Jamal was daring enough to ask his partner directly when he
got home . . . Was he angry enough to leave? As we suspected
might be the case, he wasn't at all. However, he remained
frustrated. Why wouldn't Jamal take the steps he clearly
wanted to take?

This scenario is not uncommon. He hates his job, has other
options, and genuinely seems to want to leave. So, why doesn't
he? Did he have a habit of avoiding uncomfortable thoughts or
conversations? Was his self-esteem low, and he felt this was the
best he could get? Had he been ground down by his job and
no longer felt like he had any control over what was happening
to him? There are always a myriad of possible reasons we do
things, but in Jamal's case it was – surprise, surprise – another
heuristic (sorry, not sorry, this chapter is about heuristics and
they are absolutely everywhere).

Have you ever dated someone who doesn't treat you well?
You know you should leave, but you don't because you have
been together for ten years and, well, that's a long time –
and maybe it will get better. Or have you ever watched
a terrible movie and even though you could have walked
out, you stay, moaning about what a waste of your time it
is? If you resonate with either of these, you have a flavour
of Jamal's experience and the final heuristics I am going to
share with you.

The first one is the 'sunk-cost fallacy' – the tendency to
believe we should stick at anything we have already invested

our time or money in even if it makes no other logical sense to do so. The more time or money we have invested in something, the more likely it is that we will see that thing through to the end, even if there are plenty of warning signs saying, *STOP!* The second is the 'status quo bias', the tendency for humans to keep everything the same at all times.

Jamal found that when it came to crunch time, he suddenly got cold feet. Getting cold feet just before a major life change makes sense – avoiding uncertainty helped us survive as a species. But you, Jamal and I are not in that time of life, and we need to learn to tolerate uncertainty. To do this, we looked at the pros and cons of him leaving his job, and we followed his 'what if . . .' fears all the way to their natural end, i.e. the question: 'What if I leave and it was a terrible decision?'; answer: 'Then at least I will know, and I will then apply for another job. I have money in the bank should I need to leave without the next job lined up. I could even apply for my old job, should I want to.' Then, lo and behold, he left his job for another role . . .

And . . .

. . . he hated it! He missed his old job, particularly because the boss he had clashed with left at the same time. His biggest fear – *What if I leave and it was a terrible decision?* – came true, but we had already planned for this. We didn't know if our plan would work out, but he got in touch with his old company and asked if there were any roles going. Six months down the line, he was back in his old role, with a clearer view of what he did and didn't want.

If you are thinking, *Oh my god, he should never have left*, I disagree. I could have given you an example of someone taking the leap and it all working out, which is more often than not the outcome that we achieve when we take chances in our life. But had I done that, we wouldn't have learned one of the most important lessons we can learn in life.

Most people believe that making decisions is extremely hard because we must make the perfect choice. We believe we only get one shot. In reality, very few decisions are final and there is plenty to be gained by trying new things. We can make a decision that feels right for us in the moment, try it out and if it doesn't succeed, then try something else, or even see if we can go back to where we started. Life is a process of learning. Of making good decisions, good-for-right-now decisions, and decisions that turn out not to be what we need in the long run – and that's normal, not a sign of failure.

I realize that if you leave a job or a person or move to a new city you can't guarantee that you will be able to go back to how things were before, so we shouldn't take these decisions lightly. However, to make better decisions, we need to recognize that sometimes we will make a choice based on the best information we have at that time and that it won't work out – and that is okay. There is always something else we can do.

Better decisions arise when we allow new information and statistics to educate us and to change our minds. Particularly when we realize our previous idea is no longer appropriate. The research shows, however, that a lot of us struggle with this, as people tend to beat themselves up for longer if they make a 'bad decision' after they changed their mind in the past, than if the decision had a bad outcome but they had stuck to their original idea.[11] This feature of being human is making us worse decision-makers. Be courageous enough to look for new information. Be courageous enough to change your mind. Be courageous enough to know that you can make steps that do not in the end work out.

To get to your death bed and have 'no regrets', as it were, is rarely achieved by avoiding making some hard decisions. It is more often achieved by courageously facing uncertainty and the prospect that things may not go as planned. This feels like a good moment to bring this chapter to a conclusion, and to remember our furry friend from Chapter 1. The mouse who tried and kept on trying until he got to that warm patch of ground, the victor. He didn't take the right action the first time; he kept chipping away at the task, making decision after decision to keep trying, and it paid off. This can be you.

Unsticking points

- When you feel certain that you know what you value in life and that you are making decisions that are in your best interests, you might still struggle to take the steps you need in order to make the necessary changes.
- It is helpful to get comfortable making decisions that are best for now but might change when we have better information. Many people believe they must make the perfect decision all the time. But the reality is most decisions only need to be the best decision for that moment and most are also reversible. As long as you are not making a life-or-death decision, you don't have to get it 100 per cent right the first time.

Chapter 3

Self-Sabotage

*'I decry the injustice of my wounds, only
to look down and see that I am holding a
smoking gun in one hand and a fistful of
ammunition in the other'*
—CRAIG D. LOUNSBROUGH

On 15 November 2012, Jia Jang – a thirty-year-old marketing manager living in Texas – started a seemingly strange set of behaviours that lasted 100 days and went on to change the rest of his life.

Each day, Jia asked strangers unexpected questions. He asked his local donut shop if they could make him fresh donuts that connected like the Olympic rings. To his surprise, they did it. He asked Domino's if he could deliver pizza for them (they said no), Abercrombie & Fitch if he could model for them (also no; he wasn't 'muscly enough'), Southwest Airlines if he could make the safety announcement when everyone boarded the plane (another no, as he would need to be strapped into his seat at that time, but they said he could do the welcome announcement instead), and professors at the University of Texas if he could teach one of their classes (surprisingly, a professor of communication said yes!).

Jia set out on this mission because, at thirty, he felt he hadn't done half of the things he wished to do in life. He had always wanted to be a high-flying business mogul and, growing up, he never had any doubt that he would achieve this, but for some reason, he had never got close. When he was honest with himself, he realized the cause: each time he came up with an idea or was given a significant opportunity to take a step forward, he, like so many of us, didn't take it because he was terrified of failure and rejection. Now, he needed something to change.

He found a website called rejectiontherapy.com by a Canadian entrepreneur called Jason Comely, who said you could desensitize yourself to rejection by getting rejected over and over. So, Jia set out to test the theory his own way, by aiming to get rejected 100 days in a row. Jia learned three important lessons from his experiment:

1. Rejection is survivable.
2. Sometimes, when you assume you will be rejected, you will be surprised – someone might say, 'Yeah, sure, I will make your donuts into the Olympics sign' or 'Teach my class, why not!'
3. When someone says no, you can often ask why and get an answer you didn't expect. For example, Jia knocked on a stranger's door and asked if

he could plant a flower in his garden, but the guy said no. When Jia asked why, the man explained that his dog would just dig it up, but that the lady over the road might like one. When Jia crossed the road, the lady welcomed him and his flower with open arms.

Jia's experiment was so successful that he went from being the person who didn't take chances to having a TED Talk that has amassed over 9 million views and writing a book called *Rejection Proof: How I beat fear and became invincible through 100 days of rejection*. Wow.

I'm not suggesting that we all approach a big birthday like Jia did, but there are lessons to be learned from the challenge he set himself and that illustrate the next biggest challenge that keeps us stuck. Even when we know how to change our habits and overcome our thinking biases, there is a third factor we need to look out for: self-sabotage.

Why we sabotage

The first two chapters explain how to identify which habits are creating obstacles to the life you want, how to create habits that will get you closer to where you want to be, and how to make decisions that will support that. At the end of the last chapter, we learned that sometimes we don't take action in our lives due to the status quo heuristic and sunk-cost fallacy. But there are many other reasons we may race towards a starting line and then find ourselves shuddering to a halt as we get close to crossing it, and most of them fall into the category of self-sabotage.

Self-sabotage is the term used to describe any action that we take that obstructs our ability to achieve our goals and live the way we want to. It isn't usually intentional, but, just like so many things we have discussed, is something we do to avoid what our brain believes is too threatening for us to tolerate – when the feeling of immediate threat outweighs the potential rewards that could be achieved down the line. In Jia's case, he wanted a grand life but felt he needed to avoid rejection, so his sabotage was turning down any and every opportunity that could give him what he wanted.

Sabotage can take many forms and can arise for many reasons. Sometimes we are aware we are engaging in sabotage and other times, we have no awareness at all. I see situations like this happening all the time in my clinic. People come to therapy feeling stuck, unable to move forward or take charge of their lives. They have made a decision that they want to do/have/be something, but no matter how hard they try, it never works out. On the surface this outcome seems like it could be down to chance, but when we dig a little deeper we see that, as Lounsbrough's quote puts it so well, they are holding both the smoking gun and the ammunition – they are personally responsible for shooting their plans dead in the water.

Some clients who are stuck say they want a partner, but they also fear being rejected and often don't realize that they unknowingly sabotage their chances (read: keep themselves safe from the risk of rejection) by dating people who say they don't want anything serious, or by keeping their date at arm's length. This self-sabotage is a very human thing to do.

Some clients who want to run their own business or try a new hobby but fear failure may realize that they sabotage their chances by never trying, subconsciously thinking, *If I don't try, then at least no one can say I have failed.* But, after deciding to face their fears and give whatever it is they want to do a try, they may not realize the other ways they sabotage themselves. For example, I often see people who say they want a new job but then sabotage their chances by getting drunk the night before an important interview. This is a slightly unique form of sabotage, as it performs three functions. Firstly, the alcohol masks the anxiety; secondly, it serves as a good excuse if the job is given to someone else *(I was so hungover, there really was no way I would get the job)*; and thirdly, it makes them look even better should they then go on to get the job *(It's extraordinary really – I was so hungover and STILL got the job; I must be even better than I thought).* This kind of sabotage is referred to in the research literature as 'behavioural handicapping', which is something I'll touch on again shortly.

I don't just see self-sabotage in my clinic. It's everywhere. At university, a good friend of mine, Sandrine, set up a new business at the exact time that we were meant to be revising for our exams. Looking back, she realizes the university work created extreme anxiety; the fears piled on top of her at the same rate as the notes she had yet to learn stacked up on her desk. So, she made herself impossibly busy, avoiding the emotions and the work. Until the exams came, and, well ... you can imagine what happened then. Nowadays, she clears her calendar when there is an upcoming deadline so that there can be no excuse. However, she has noticed a new issue arising: whenever she sits down to work, fatigue washes over her. She has the sudden urge to lie down and rest, even though, only a few minutes before, when she was doing an activity she enjoyed, she felt as fresh as a daisy.

When we want to avoid doing something, even if this desire is outside of our field of awareness, it seems that our brain will always find a way to avoid that very thing. In Sandrine's case the fatigue provided her with a believable excuse to avoid her fears. But, the good news is, she is savvy to her patterns and so, instead of buying into the feelings, she sees the tiredness as a sign she must be feeling overwhelmed, and deals with this by breaking her tasks down into bite-sized chunks that she can tackle one step at a time.

Can you think of an area of your life where you are feeling stuck, that may have something to do with your own actions? Did you take on a house-painting project the weekend you had to hand in your book draft? Or, is that just me?! By the end of this chapter, you will be able to identify the whys and wheres of your personal sabotage, so that you can stop getting in the way of the things you truly want in life.

Unsticking point

- We sometimes feel stuck in our lives as we set out to achieve a goal and find we can never quite achieve it. Not because we can't but because we sabotage our own chances at happiness or success, in order to avoid difficult emotions such as fear, pain, shame, discomfort and sometimes boredom.

Blowing it all up

We don't just sabotage by avoiding the fears associated with trying and failing. We also sabotage to avoid the fears and emotional pain that can arise once *we are deep into a situation we hoped for*. We see it in the papers, whenever we read about a politician or celebrity that has destroyed their home life through substance abuse or an affair that ended in the public eye. While we can't know why each person does what they do, I would hazard a guess that many famous cases of self-sabotage link to fear and painful feelings. Fears of failure and rejection. Fears of irrelevance. The pain of loneliness and other kinds of hurt that people wish to avoid at all costs. And, in some cases, it may be related to power, and other expectations linked to the role they find themselves in – a point we will discuss in more detail in Chapter 5. The important thing to note, however, is that whenever sabotage strikes, there is always a way to overcome it. It does not have to destroy us.

Help, I'm stuck

'I really want a family, but every time I get taken in by a foster family something goes wrong and I get sent back into care. There is something wrong with me. I used to fear that nobody would want me but now I know it isn't just a fear. It's a fact. I am going to be stuck here forever.'

—The devastating words of BEN,
who was fourteen years old

'He has had so many foster opportunities. They always
seem to start out okay. In fact, in the beginning, it seems
like a dream as they get on so well. Then, when everyone
starts to think, "This is it!", everything starts to fall
apart. Fights start in the family; the school starts sending
home reports that he is acting out there too. The problems
escalate until he gets sent back to us. The pattern is the
same every time. We're stuck.'

—ANNIE, Ben's social worker

At fourteen, Ben had been coming to the clinic for many years and our team knew him well. If you knew him, Ben was the kind of awkward teen who, after a huge growth spurt, seemed a little unsteady in his new-found height, his limbs seemingly everywhere and not always under his control. He was also sweet and eager to please, chatting away, asking if he could help make tea (as long as there were no other teenagers around to witness this vulnerable and open part of his character). To people who didn't know him, Ben was guarded, and his shy demeanour, mixed with his height, was sometimes (mis)interpreted as intimidating. As long as you took your time and introduced yourself to him calmly, the teen who loved biting the ends of KitKats before dunking one end into his tea to use it as a straw, while asking you about your day, would re-emerge. Every time he met a new potential foster family, it was only a matter of time before they truly cared about him.

The first couple of times Ben's foster placement fell through, many variables were blamed – 'It was his first time meeting a new family', 'The chemistry wasn't right', 'He was too far away from his siblings, who were in different foster homes'. Now, six families in, there was a distinct pattern that could not be ignored. It was time to think a little differently about what was going on.

When we care about something more than anything in the world, huge pressure and a great deal of anxiety can build around it. Maybe you can think of a time when you wanted to tell someone that you care about them, but every time you tried to do it you panicked and ended up saying something flippant and cold instead, as the vulnerability made you feel defensive. Or maybe you really wanted to have a conversation with someone you deem extremely important at work, but when you finally got a chance to speak to them, you became clumsy, giggling inappropriately, acting totally out of character. Maybe you wanted to start your own business but found that you couldn't get anything done, as the pressure you put on yourself to make it perfect made your mind go blank every time you tried to sit down and start.

What did Ben want more than anything in the world? A family. When Ben was brought into a new foster home, it would go smoothly at the beginning. He was himself. But, as he started to care about the family, and/or they clearly showed affection for him in return, deep fears started to arise – *What if these people kick me out too?* The prediction of this outcome caused panic, and his emotions became harder for him to manage, resulting in outbursts of anger. None of this was sabotage; it was overwhelm.

The anger led to shame, which made him panic more, and his behaviour became increasingly erratic. When the foster family and later the school tried to talk to Ben about his behaviour, he felt like his worst fears were being realized – *Everyone thinks there is something wrong with me, I am about to get sent back to care*. He became so convinced he would be kicked out he stopped trying to improve things; he self-sabotaged, turning purely to behaviours that would get him in trouble. Why would he do such a thing?

Like Jia, Ben had a fear of rejection, but instead of turning down opportunities, he blew them up. His fear of rejection made him feel out of control and certain he was about to be abandoned again, which was unbearable, so he remedied it in his own way: *If I act as badly as I can, the ending will at least be swift and on my own terms.*

Ben thought *he* was the problem. He was not the problem. His experience of being abandoned as a child had led to a fear of being rejected that was so overwhelming that any time something went well, he was convinced it would soon fall apart. Subsequently he escalated his behaviour in ways that, unfortunately, made sure it did. And the moment it did, he immediately forgot that he had taken charge of the ending, seeing only the proof that his deepest fears were true – *No one stuck around, so it must be that no one could ever want me*. This is a classic example of the sabotage cycle.

The sabotage cycle

Deep belief/story
e.g. 'I am unlovable', 'I am a failure'

Trigger
e.g. thinking about something you want or
need to do, or something you want to be part
of that triggers your deep fear belief, such as
going on a date or starting a new job

Feeling
e.g. discomfort or something more arises
that says 'don't do it, it will be too much/
too dangerous for you' or 'it will go wrong'

Sabotage
any act that takes you back to a feeling of
safety and control – usually engaged in without
conscious awareness of the reason behind it

Deep belief/story confirmed as your
situation does not change

Self-sabotage takes away acute discomfort. It also creates situations in which only our deepest fears and oldest beliefs can be proved. Jia saw his age as proof that he was a failure because he hadn't done what he had always wanted to do. The person who doesn't try at work, so as never to fail at the thing they care about, reaches a point where they feel like a failure as nothing ever changes. And so, the cycle continues.

The solution for Ben was not 100 days of rejection, as each day of his life to date had felt like this for him. Instead, he needed compassion and support to understand why he felt and acted the way he did. He needed someone to show him how to express his emotions in ways that were constructive, and he needed a family who could help him to feel safe. The most important part of this process was teaching him how self-sabotage works and how it gets us stuck. Only later, when it felt manageable enough, could he face his fears and learn that he could overcome them. When he went to his next family, he told them on day one that when he fears abandonment his behaviours change, but that this time, he planned to tell people his fears rather than acting them out. A huge, life-changing step.

If anything in this chapter resonates with you, please remember that beating yourself up for self-sabotage is not the answer. Knowing why it is happening, and what to do about it, is.

Unsticking points

- Sabotage is a way people seek safety. It eases our pain short term and always confirms our fear long term.
- Sabotage causes us to feel stuck not only because it stops us from taking chances; it can also cause us to

act in ways that ensure that the chances we have can't come to fruition.

- We usually become aware of sabotage when we acknowledge that, like Jia and Ben, there are patterns arising in our life that we can simply no longer ignore.

Are you stuck because you are self-sabotaging?

- **Ask yourself if you relate to any of the examples you have come across so far in this chapter.** Do you tend to avoid things that you could fail at? Do you put yourself down in front of others? Do you set tests for your loved ones? Do you criticize yourself relentlessly rather than focus on what you could learn from the inevitable mistakes you make (because we all make mistakes)? Or do you have affairs whenever the going gets tough and wonder why everything always collapses around you, and see this as proof that relationships fail? Maybe you buy books like this one, never get round to doing the exercises and then wonder why things never change, seeing the lack of change as proof that it can't?

- **Once you have found something you might consider sabotage, write down all the possible factors that may have caused you to act in a way that helped you to seek safety in the short term but caused problems in the long term.** As there

---

may be many reasons, don't be afraid to list them all. Over time, you will get to know which reasons are a common theme for you (e.g. if you avoid new activities, is it because you fear failure? Or because you fear being judged by others? Do you put yourself down, thinking that getting to the punchline first will remove some of that judgement? If you set tests for your loved ones, is it because you fear you are unlovable and need assurance that people who say they care about you really mean it?

- **Spend the next twenty-four hours looking for moments that could count as sabotage.** It could be any moment you engage in what we called a 'bad habit' in the first chapter. Or it could be something new, like noticing that your perfectionism makes you want to opt out of an activity as you can't be sure you will do it perfectly, or noticing a need for control, which causes you not to delegate tasks to people who could share your workload.

Remember, these awareness exercises are entry-level mindfulness practices. Mindful awareness is not only helpful in managing habits and heuristics; it will also be your friend when it comes to sabotage, as it helps you get curious about your patterns and choose a new way forward.

Pseudo-sabotage

An important public service announcement: not all patterns in life come down to safety-seeking behaviour. Here are three other situations that often get confused with self-sabotage.

1. The Big Five

Certain personality traits are 40–60 per cent heritable (passed through our DNA). These include agreeableness (how cooperative, trusting, compassionate and likeable you are/aim to be); conscientiousness (how industrious, achievement-orientated, dependable and orderly you are); extraversion (how sociable, enthusiastic, ambitious and assertive you are); neuroticism (how anxious and volatile your emotions are, and how you cope); and openness to experience (how imaginative, open, nonconforming and intellectually curious you are). These traits are thought to be measurable through the Big Five Personality Test, and knowing about them can be extremely helpful.

I have a friend, Mayowa, who gets overexcited about every new person he meets and dates. He discusses his latest love interest as if they are a precious jewel that no one has ever seen the likes of before – but, without fail, a few weeks later, the date has been relegated to just another pebble on the beach. One night over a glass of wine, a mutual friend told Mayowa that he had a history of putting high levels of effort into new relationships and then disappearing once the novelty wore off. He was up for discussing this and we queried whether what we noticed was solely a coincidence and not a pattern at all, a traditional form of self-sabotage, or something else, like his personality traits. He took the test and it seemed it was the latter. He was high in 'openness to experience' and low in 'agreeableness' and 'conscientiousness', meaning he rarely felt the drive towards cooperation or connecting with people further once it no longer felt new.

Upon seeing this, another friend, Amy, who was initially sceptical, said she was going to take the personality test. The look on her face said she planned to do this to prove to us all that the tests were nonsense. So, we topped up our glasses while she completed the questionnaire. Amy was agog. The findings explained something she had long been curious about. She had a history of achieving goals and working her socks off but found that, at other times, and seemingly without warning, she would struggle with deadlines to the point where she could barely motivate herself to do any work at all. She had been curious as to whether this was a procrastination issue or another form of sabotage, but the results explained this conundrum very clearly. She was low on 'conscientiousness' and high on 'agreeableness', which meant that she felt driven when other people were involved or when missing a deadline would risk putting someone else out, but when no one else was involved, she hit the brakes and the finish line remained out of reach.

Knowing your personality traits does not mean you get to say, 'Well, it's just who I am, take it or leave it,' as Mayowa said, while leaning back in his seat and putting his feet up on the chair nearest to him, to the resounding response of 'no, no, no' from the rest of us! It offers an opportunity to play to your strengths to reach your goals. For example, if you are like Mayowa and low in conscientiousness and agreeableness, but high in openness to experience, you can use your strength (openness to experience) to motivate behaviours that make you more prosocial. You could use your love of gathering knowledge to motivate you to learn about positive, reciprocal social behaviours, why they please others, and what you in turn could gain from long-standing relationships. Or you could suggest learning new activities together to the people you date. If you are like Amy, the person who gives up the ghost when going at it alone, you can use your strengths (high agreeability) to help you focus more, ensuring you work with a group of people you respect and want to collaborate with to keep you motivated.

2. Repeating patterns learned in childhood

Sometimes, what looks like sabotage is purely learned behaviour – habits we picked up at an early age. An obvious example: if you saw your parents drown their sorrows in alcohol, you may now behave similarly whenever difficult emotions arise. Less obvious examples: if you saw your parents swing between loving and berating the people closest to them, you may notice that as an adult, once you get close to someone new, a spiteful side arises. Or if you saw adults leave when the going got tough in their relationships, you may want to jump ship the moment things start to seem less blissful than they did when you started dating. While each of these outcomes have the possibility of getting in the way of your desired life, they are not traditional sabotage. You are not seeking safety in these situations; you are performing routines. In Chapter 5, we will focus on patterns arising across generations, and how to truly overcome them, in more detail.

3. Skill deficits

Sometimes behaviour that looks like self-sabotage is an indicator that you need to learn a new skill. For example, many relationships fail when the people involved haven't learned how to communicate clearly what they need, like and don't like from the people in their lives. And some 'only children' notice that as adults they want to opt out of the race when competition arises, uninclined to fight for the top spot as they never learned healthy (or unhealthy) competition growing up.

Like the iceberg that only shows 10 per cent of its mass above the surface, a behaviour we can observe may have a mass of reasons beneath. Do not assume that all patterns in your life, or behaviours that you see that get in the way of your goals, are self-sabotage. Use the box below to get clear on this.

Three steps to find out where you may be going wrong

When you notice a pattern that is getting you stuck that might be sabotage:

1. **Go online and take a Big Five Personality Test.**
   Look at what your strengths are, consider what you

---

need to bolster, and ask yourself how you can use the information to build the life you want.

2. **Ask yourself when you first started to notice this pattern of behaviour.** If the answer is as far back as you can remember, see if you remember seeing anyone else engaging in behaviours like these at another time in your life. If you find something that you saw others doing, treat it as though it is a 'bad habit' that needs replacing. Choose a new belief and think about the cues you will use to recognize when it could happen again, and what you will do instead. Then, head to Chapter 5 to get really clear on what *not* to do.

3. **Ask yourself if it could be happening due to a lack of skills in that area.** If the answer is yes, decide how you can address this to get unstuck.

Unsticking point

- Behaviours that look like sabotage might actually not be sabotage at all and could link to other things, including personality traits and what we learned when we were children.

Sneaky sabotage

When people start getting savvy about sabotage, the next question is usually: 'How much of this is sabotage and how much is just circumstance?' My answer is always, 'If you don't know where to start, it can be helpful to assume it's 50/50 (50 per cent you and 50 per cent everything else) and work from there.' This helps people who over-blame themselves to see that it takes two to tango and that they are not responsible for everything, and also helps people who usually apportion all responsibility to others to see their part.

Help, I'm stuck

> 'Which parts of my trouble dating are down to my
> behaviour, and which are solely chance, i.e. I haven't met
> the right person yet?'

—ZOLA, 37

Zola is hyperindependent, smart as a whip, hilarious and extremely chic. That last part may sound superficial, but I promise, it's important. Zola came to therapy purely because she wanted to. She had no acute symptoms that needed managing. No obvious trauma from her past that she needed to face. She simply believed therapy was a good thing to do if you wanted to live well.

Zola was fascinated with people's behaviour and curious to

find out if there were any patterns in her life that needed tackling that she was as yet unaware of. Sometimes I suspected that she simply wanted what my own therapist calls 'someone to watch the show with her'. This is not a judgmental statement; it is something I and so many others are looking for. It means wanting someone to bear witness to our existence; someone to share the highs and lows of life with; someone who really gets us and is willing to sit with us through it all.

One day I suggested this might be something that would resonate with her and asked if she had that with anyone outside of therapy. She shared that she didn't, and confessed she was ashamed to admit that she really wanted to meet someone. Ashamed because she thought it embarrassing to want love and a partner. Strong people, she believed, didn't have such needs. They were happier on their own. This was a limiting belief; a form of sabotage that told her never to discuss her desires or needs as it would make her seem weak in some way.

As she got more comfortable discussing this, she shared that she had been dating almost consistently for a decade and was starting to panic that she might never meet the right person, but at the same time was determined not to settle for just anyone. We spent some of our sessions answering the key question of hers outlined in the quote above – *Which parts of my trouble dating are down to my behaviour, and which are solely chance?* We started with my usual 50/50 starting position and moved from there, listing reasons previous dates had gone awry.

Clear examples that were not sabotage: dates that ended as they simply didn't get on; dates that ended because they didn't have a shared view of the future (e.g. she knew she didn't want children but the date did); dates that ended because once the lust had faded, it was clear they had no deeper connection.

Clear examples linked to 'her': times she turned down dates for fear they wouldn't go well; times she listed all the things she disliked about herself to her new dates, thinking this was a vulnerable share that would bring them closer together, but instead felt more like she was trying to put the other person off her.

There were more subtle moments that constituted sabotage too. One day she told me she went on dates in her pyjamas – not the chic daytime pyjama suits she sometimes wore to our sessions, but her Christmas PJs and a moth-eaten jumper. Her reason for this was that 'they need to like me whether I am dressed up or down, warts and all'. I understood her sentiment. For too long, women have been told they have to present themselves in a certain way in order to be eye-catching and appealing for others, and this wears thin. Why can't we just be who we are and people like us for that? It's empowering to have a 'fuck it' spirit about these things, and as a feminist I whole-heartedly agree with this. However, as a therapist, I know that lots of people who fear rejection or believe they will be rejected go on dates and sabotage them before they start, by – for example – not making an effort. This sounded like my client.

Imagine going on a first date with someone who has made an effort, vs someone who looks like they've just rolled out of bed, and consider the subtle signals their presentation sends to you. Making an effort or not can be the difference between sending the message 'I am confident, I like to look after myself and I thought this date was worth making an effort for', and, well . . . potentially the opposite.

My client said that she noticed she didn't feel her best when she went on her PJ dates and found she was a little defensive, ready to justify her choice of attire – *Men always want women to be perfect and I am sick of it! This is further proof of the patriarchy.* She left the house feeling empowered but arrived at the date ready for a fight. When we investigated this behaviour further, she had a eureka moment. 'Oh my god, I always worry that the date won't go well, and I have found another way to ensure that it doesn't before it even starts!'

Not everyone who goes on dates in their PJs is self-sabotaging, and I would not dream of criticizing people for their sartorial choices. I simply knew my client well and could see that this was out of character for her and fitted in with her other patterns of sabotage while dating. I tell you this story, as safety-seeking behaviour can be very sneaky. Like a wolf dressed in sheep's clothing (or pyjamas), we can easily miss it if we aren't aware of our beliefs and fears.

Unsticking points

- It is only when we radically face the possibility that we may have more agency over our patterns than it seems, that we can identify and change the barriers we create for ourselves.
- Sometimes it takes playing with ideas that seem like they can't be sabotage to find the things that are. This might be easier to do with a non-judgemental friend, or with a therapist.

Getting to know which fears may cause you to sabotage

1. **Write down what you believe to be true about your potential, lovability, employability and ability to effect action in your life.** Do you fear you don't have potential in any of these areas? If so, it's okay; we just need to know what fears to look out for. Also, if you notice that you sometimes think one thing about yourself and in other moments think the opposite, that is normal – many of us only feel like a failure or unlovable from time to time. If this is you, put 'I sometimes fear that . . .'

2. **Return to your list of potential moments of sabotage from the last exercise and ask yourself if there are any moments the fears you described above were confirmed? And if the answer is yes, can you think of anything you may have done to cause that to happen?** I know this can feel scary to consider, so I will go first . . .

I want a connected group of friends, but deep down often fear I may not be lovable enough for people to stick around once they get to know me. I fear these things because of experiences I had when young. I see that there is a pattern in my life of meeting people and hitting it off instantly, but then the next few times we meet up, the initial spark cools off and I am sure it is because they discovered I wasn't quite as great as I first seemed. With hindsight, I can see that when I first meet people there is no risk; I am not invested in them and so I feel free to be as 'myself' as I like. But once I am invested, my fear arises and I back away. I say no to events and act aloof, and then wonder why the initial spark of the relationship has fizzled out. Your turn . . .

3. **Once you have identified potential sabotage, write what you will need to pay attention to going forward** (to identify cues for this behaviour) and what you will do instead. For example, in my case, I started to pay attention to my habits around interacting with new friends. When I thought, *They aren't texting or chatting* and felt panicked and shut down, I used this as a cue to practice the STOP technique, and then I asked myself whether I had been initiating conversation at all. Often, they hadn't contacted me as I hadn't given them cause to! In response to this, I then text those people. Then I practice self-compassion. I do this because overcoming sabotage involves understanding why we do what we do, choosing a new behaviour, and deciding on other ways to meet the emotional needs that drive the sabotage in the first place. For me, I manage my fear of rejection with self-compassion; what will you do to support yourself through your fears?

4. **Return to your list of goals and the habits that you wish to bring into your life.** Circle any of them that your fears may cause you to sabotage and decide what you will do to manage this.

5. **Set up an experiment to test your new behaviour and see what happens.** Jia set out to get rejected for 100 days. I set out by continuously initiating interactions with the people I usually pulled away from. While my anxiety went up during this period, so did the volume of contact I had with my new friends! See what you can do to test out your new behaviour.

Remember, you have the skills from Chapter 1 that could be used here too. For example, if you don't feel quite ready to test out your new behaviour, you might be in the pre-contemplative or contemplative stage of the change cycle and can therefore ask: 'What will happen if I don't try?' What are the pros and cons of staying the same or trying something new? And you can use the technique from Chapter 2 that I used with Jamal, of following your 'what if . . .' thoughts all the way to the end, e.g. 'What will I do if the worst-case scenario happens? How would I cope?' Appendix 3 has a step-by-step guide to challenging your fears, so head there now if you want to do further work in this area.

Identity and the saboteur

As you can see, fears are a core driver of true self-sabotage, but so are negative beliefs. Perhaps the most talked-about negative beliefs that cause sabotage are iterations of 'I'm not good enough', 'There is only one space at the top', 'I need to wait for the perfect moment before I can start' or 'I'm always going to be rejected' – all of which mean we are unlikely to push through the difficult moments or will give up before we start. Worrying about everything that can go wrong as a means of being better prepared is an erroneous belief that will either have us panicking about something that never happens, meaning we suffered for no reason, or make us doubly miserable, as we spend time stressed out about the terrible things that could happen and then reliving that stress when it does happen. On that last point, there are obviously caveats. It is smart to prepare for potential risks in life, and when an errant worry burrows its way into your brain, it can be extraordinarily helpful to decide what exactly you would do to tackle that fear should it come to pass. However, in most cases, when we believe that worrying is truly useful, we do not tackle it in this way. We sit and generate all the worst things that could happen, one fear leading to the next, disappearing into a hole of 'what ifs' that go on and on without solution.

And there are other beliefs that are rarely talked about and that are well known to cause sabotage.

In Chapter 2 we learned about stereotypes and the halo effect (judging someone's entire personality based on one part of their identity). Now we are going to discuss how stereotypes about our identity can cause us to self-sabotage through three different means.

1. Stereotypes tell us who is meant to do what and when, meaning we limit ourselves when we try to act outside of a stereotype

Did you know there are gendered differences in the way we sabotage? For example:

- Women often believe they should get another qualification before applying for a job that they may already meet the necessary criteria (the sabotage: not applying for a job they could get due to a fear that they aren't qualified enough as they are), while men are more likely to apply for positions they don't have the qualifications for.
- Men are more likely to engage in 'behavioural self-handicapping' than women. Remember the example of the person who would get drunk the night before the interview that they really cared about? This is the kind of sabotage that means they have triple protection (anxiety management, an excuse for failing and a reason for others to be even more impressed with them should that failure not occur). People of all genders do this, but usually to a lesser extent than men, and on those occasions, with something made up – i.e. rather than actively getting drunk or withdrawing their effort, they may say they had something happen that isn't true but fits the bill, e.g. *I am struggling as I didn't sleep/because I am feeling unwell.*

These differences arise due to the way each gender is socialized as children and then treated as adults. For example, men are typically socialized to compete and show their prowess through skill. They are usually taught that they are meant to be leaders and that their ability is natural (instead of something you work for). This mixture means that people socialized as men are 1) more likely to believe they deserve to be in higher roles, 2) more afraid of failure, which they don't necessarily believe can be avoided through harder work (as they have been taught that you either have the talent or you don't), and 3) more likely to engage in behavioural self-handicapping, due to the way boys rarely learn to share their fears and manage them constructively.[1]

People socialized as women, on the other hand, learn to believe that they must work twice as hard as men to do the same things and be seen as equally good. This means that they are more likely to double down on work in order to achieve, and undervalue the skills they currently have. Interestingly, research shows that when a man fails in the workplace, it is often explained away as 'bad luck' or due to a 'lack of effort' on their part, whereas when women fail at the same task in a similar way, the outcome is usually attributed to ability – 'the task was too hard for her' – and this keeps the cycle alive.[2]

2. The fear that a stereotype is true causes us to make mistakes

When groups of people are stereotyped (for example, if they are believed to have little innate ability at something), research shows that time and time again many people will prove that to be true – but not because it is true.

Remember Jamal, who was struggling to leave his job? During our time working together, we encountered another reason he was stuck. After he returned to his job (the one he temporarily left) he started a training programme that included IQ testing. He had no problem with the difficulty of the tasks on the training programme and never struggled when it came to the pressures of deadlines or projects at work, but the moment the IQ test date loomed on the horizon, he suddenly became too busy to prepare for the tests. I initially thought he was doing this due to the gendered socialization issues we just discussed, but when I put this to him, he shook his head. It was another stereotype that got in the way. Growing up, he had heard people say that 'Black people are not innately smart' more times than he could count. And now, he wasn't just about to take any old test; he was about to be tested on his intelligence. A small voice in the back of his mind was asking, *What if those people were right?* He had tried to ignore the thought, but then when he picked up the information about the test, he found there were lots of things he couldn't easily remember, and interpreted this as a sign that the voice was correct, and everyone was about to find out that the stereotype was true. There is a name for the experience of being in a situation where a stereotype about your social group could end up being proven: 'stereotype threat' – a common consequence of which is, you guessed it, self-sabotage.

'Stereotype threat' challenges people's identity and self-worth and uses up valuable psychological resources, preventing them from succeeding at the task at hand. When the person notices they are struggling (as we pay attention to what we fear) the stereotype threat increases. This anxiety affects ability, and sabotage can creep in to manage the discomfort.

This is exactly what happened to Jamal. In order to get over this, we looked for the examples in his life and history that proved his fears about his IQ and the stereotype to be true and also false (there were many more examples for this stereotype being false, as there always is when you investigate your fears and the stereotypes you have learned), worked on mindfulness to acknowledge negative thoughts but also let them go (knowing thoughts are not truths), and then looked for positive examples of people who challenged the stereotype and could act as mental role models. Slowly his anxiety ebbed, and he was able to take the test feeling like himself.

3. Stereotypes affect the choices we make

There isn't just a stereotype threat. There is stereotype embodiment too, which usually happens when a stereotype doesn't pertain to you when you first hear it but does later on. Ageing is a great example of this.

Did you know that very recent research shows that having a positive image of ageing increases the likelihood that you will live longer and stay physically healthy, and also decreases the likelihood of you developing dementia, even in those who have a gene predisposing them to the disease?[3]

When we grow up hearing stereotypes about old age, we think of these comments being about other people. But, once we reach the age the comments refer to, it is as if the stereotype is activated, affecting how we treat ourselves, think about ourselves and the decisions we make. Negative stereotypes are likely to make us interpret normal lapses in attention (such as forgetting where you put your keys or struggling to remember information during times of stress) as a sign that our memory is going, or to assume the days we feel stiff (which could occur simply as we did too much exercise, or because we need to do more exercise and have spent too much time sitting down) as a sign of a loss of mobility. This in turn makes us more likely to be less active, healthy or adventurous as we think, *I am too old for that.*

Obviously, there are many unforeseen events that can harm us, such as sudden illness, but sometimes we sabotage our chance at happiness because we simply don't believe health, happiness and success can be for us. This can happen with any stereotype. The upside of the research that brought us these findings is that it showed us a simple but powerful solution that each of us can use to overcome the link between stereotyping and self-sabotage. It showed that when we look for exceptions to the stereotypes and hold them as our image of what is possible for us in life, we are more likely to defy the stereotypes.

Unsticking point

- Stereotypes and other fears about the self can lead us to sabotage our chances because they cause anxiety and limit what we think we can do.

What to do if fears and stereotypes are affecting you

1. **Write down each aspect of your identity that you think is important** and list any stereotype you have heard linked to that part of your identity (e.g. 'Women are less able than men', 'Men must always know what to do'). Ask yourself if there have ever been times where these stereotypes have caused you to avoid taking an opportunity, stop trying or feel anxious in any way. If this task seems too abstract, and no answers come to mind, instead keep a log of your self-talk for the next twenty-four hours. Pay specific attention to moments where you big yourself up and talk yourself down. Capture any time you tell yourself, 'you never . . .', 'you always . . .', or anything negative in relation to trying something new. This will help you understand the self-sabotaging nature of your self-talk, and the beliefs that may be holding you back.

2. **Return to your list of values and goals.** Are there any negative beliefs or fears that link to your identity or personal ability, that arise when you think about striving for those goals?

3. **Challenge the belief and/or stereotype.** Consider the evidence for it (if any) and ask if it is simply a thought and nothing more.

4. **Look for examples** of times when you have defied this belief/stereotype and/or people in the world who have done this.

5. **If you believe there is something you are bad at, plan for how to get better at that thing.** Maybe you believe you are bad at interviews; if so, research interview processes, do practice questions, swat up. Do not buy into the limiting belief that ability cannot be learned. Everything is a muscle, whether you are breaking a habit of a lifetime, such as reaching for cookies when stressed, overcoming the draw of heuristics when making a big decision, or learning not to buy into the critical voice that says you will never succeed.

6. **Focus on mastering the thing you want to work on.** Practice, practice, practice.

7. **Look for areas of your life where the stereotype affects you most** (e.g. at work, in relationships, etc.) and then look for a supportive community who share the same experiences.

8. **Consider an alter ego for a short period.** This is a fun tip that has been shown to work. Kids who pretend to be superheroes are more likely to do the things that scare them, and do them well, than when not in a superhero role. Some drag queens talk about their drag persona offering an outlet to experience and play at an aspect of their identity that is perhaps not allowed either by others in their

personal lives, or by themselves at that time (as they internalized the belief that 'men must never be women, never be feminine'), allowing them to decide over time which parts of this persona could be incorporated into their own lives. When I set out working for myself, I went by 'Dr Soph'. She isn't me. She is the name of the woman who puts herself (rather bravely, the real me thinks) into public spaces each day sharing psychology and beliefs. She is brave; she faces her fears; she is eloquent. She gives me the strength to do the job I do. Who could be your alter ego? How would it defy the stereotype that is stopping you from trying something? Over time, and as you discover the evidence that you can face your fears and succeed, you can decide whether to let the alter ego go.

Believing we deserve change

You now have the tools to identify what you believe in and what you want, and the three main ways you might get in the way of achieving these things (through bad habits, misleading heuristics, and sabotage). You also have the know-how to overcome each of these challenges, but there's more to it than that.

Knowing about self-sabotage – and having the tools to stop it in its tracks – is key to getting and staying unstuck in life, but you won't get very far unless you believe you deserve a better life. Having high self-esteem means you believe in your worth. Low self-esteem, on the other hand, keeps you believing that you are going to fail and can affect our behaviour in interesting ways. For example, we may interpret everything that is wrong as our fault (*They are mad at me; it's probably because I am annoying or I did a bad job*), and when things go right, we may actively start devaluing that person or thing (*If they think I am good, then there must be something wrong with them, I should probably leave*).

The masochistic thing about humans is that we gain a perverse sense of satisfaction when we find out our fears and beliefs are true – 'I knew they didn't love me', 'I knew I shouldn't have bothered trying', 'I knew I couldn't make a change in my life'. Somehow the most painful things we can tell ourselves leave us comforted that we were right all along. The Renaissance painter Michelangelo certainly knew this, as is evidenced by a poem of his, whose opening lines are: 'I get happiness from my dejection, and these disturbances give me rest.'[4] But how can pain bring us relief? It may be because pushing against the limits of what makes us feel comfortable and worrying about what will happen if we try puts us in a state of stress. When everything falls apart, this stress is removed and we experience a feeling of relief. It could also be because of a discrepancy between our expectations and our reality; if you expect something to fail and it starts to work out, the discrepancy, even when positive, causes anxiety to escalate even further, as it did in Ben's example. It may be because we identify so strongly with certain roles or aspects of our lives – such as being the single friend, the person always hunting for a job, the struggling artist who believes that success is a form of selling out – that doing well threatens our sense of self, and, again, finding we were right bolsters relief that we know ourselves. It may also be because when we are proved right, even when it comes after a fight or another high-stress situation, adrenaline and dopamine increase in the brain, improving our mood, making us feel more motivated and more dominant, if only for a short time before the realization that nothing has changed strikes again.

When you take into account the discomfort that comes from being uncertain about how our efforts will pan out, plus the status quo and confirmation bias that cause us to want to stay the same at all times and also interpret the outcomes of our efforts in ways that confirm our fear thoughts, not to mention the determination so many of us have to avoid experiences that make us uncomfortable and/or afraid, no wonder self-sabotage is rife.

Before we get into how to improve our self-esteem, we need to know exactly what it is, as so many people I know think (wrongly) that it is confidence.

Have you ever met someone who looked like they were killing it on paper – they're so good at their job, loved by many, always in control of any scenario they find themselves in – and then found out they were deeply insecure, despite their confident exterior? It's very common. Confidence simply means you have faith in your abilities, but not necessarily that you have self-esteem.

Self-esteem means believing in your worth. It means appreciating yourself regardless of what is happening in your life, what you are or aren't good at, or what flaws you perceive you have.

When you have high self-esteem, you are likely to believe you deserve to be treated well in relationships, making you able to ask for what you want and need. You are likely to believe you can make good decisions, such as leaving people who don't treat you with the respect you deserve. You can be realistic about your abilities and your shortcomings without overly criticizing yourself and are therefore likely to bounce back quickly from difficult times.

Can you see how this is different to confidence?

My confidence in my ability as a psychologist doesn't mean that I feel good about myself all the time. I don't always feel worthy when I meet a new friend or lover or look in the mirror and see a 'perceived flaw'.

When we worry we aren't good enough or don't feel accepting of who we are (low self-esteem), we often try to solve this problem by buying new clothes to impress others, working harder at our jobs, going on a diet or doing another activity that we think will make us feel more confident in a certain area. We try to boost our esteem by boosting our confidence. This makes sense, and it does often work in the short term. A new outfit can make you feel like a million bucks. A finished piece of highly praised work can make you feel a little taller. However, these feelings are short-lived. As a teenager I wondered why these experiences didn't make me feel surer of myself or more worthy of love. I also wondered why, the moment the glow wore off, my confidence wore off too. I know I am not the only person who feels this way, because I work with people in my clinic, every day, who exude confidence in certain areas of life and get a buzz every time they achieve a new success that reinforces their excellence in a particular way, but who struggle with feeling truly worthy, particularly when the post-success buzz wears off.

So, if confidence doesn't sustainably boost self-esteem, what do we do? We focus on the actual underpinnings of esteem.

Exercise to boost self-esteem

Self-esteem is made up of self-confidence, a sense of belonging and identity, and feelings of security and competence. If you want to boost your self-esteem, don't give up on trying to improve at activities that please you, as a confidence boost is not a bad place to start. However, also make sure you concentrate on these other key areas too.

Security
Ask yourself: 'Do I feel secure in my career/relationships/lifestyle at the moment?' If not, what needs to change? Self-esteem is not only an inside job; it also depends on us having a good support network that shows us continuous care, so consider the people in your life and how they make you feel.

Identity
Ask yourself: 'Do I feel like I am sure of who I am?' If you have already done the exercise from Chapter 2 to work out your values, you may already have a sense of the qualities of life that are important to you. If you don't feel sure of who you are, start there.

Belonging

Do you feel like you belong – in your social life and at work? Do you feel like the people around you support you and affirm you? Who makes you feel most supported and cared for? We view ourselves through the eyes of others, so if we can see affection in our friends and support network, we are more likely to believe we are 'good' people. Start to weed out the people who undermine you – tell them that you are not okay with being criticized and ask for what you need instead, or simply move on. Seek out people who are not afraid to be flawed and who love you for your perceived flaws too.

Competence

Are you kind to yourself? Are you able to think calmly and clearly when stressors arise or does your brain terrify you with thoughts of things that often don't end up happening? If you are hypercritical to yourself and know you get caught in many negative thinking patterns, you will benefit from starting a self-compassion practice, learning how to challenge your negative thought patterns and tendency to believe that things will go wrong. These steps require a little more explanation, so let's start with a simple compassion practice, such as asking yourself: 'How would I treat a friend in this position?' Offer yourself the words and actions you would offer them instead of the nasty words our inner critic reserves just for us.

Self-compassion doesn't get rid of painful emotions; it instead strengthens the regions of the brain associated with hope, connection, love and reward. If you want to know more about this, I wrote a whole chapter on the inner critic, and also one on self-compassion, in my first book, *A Manual for Being Human*.

Unsticking points

- The main causes of self-sabotage are perfectionism, self-criticism, fear of rejection and failure, thinking you aren't enough or are undeserving, believing a stereotype about your social group, feeling out of control or uncertain about your identity.
- To get unstuck you have to believe you deserve change, and working on your self-esteem can help you achieve this.

What if it all goes wrong by going right?

This chapter is a bit of a downer, isn't it? All this focus on fear – of failure, rejection and not being deserving of a better life – might lead you to believe that sabotage always comes from a lack of self-belief. This isn't the case. There is a cause of self-sabotage that seems counter to everything we have discussed so far – the fear of success.

Sometimes we fear succeeding as, deep down, we know we don't really want the thing we are fighting for. Honestly, I can't tell you how many times I have seen people procrastinate over and over or do something that causes them not to be able to achieve something that was supposedly their dream, and then later realize they don't actually want to do that thing; it was their parents'/friends'/society's idea. I have also seen people sabotage because they have conflicting views of what they want and need, e.g. 'What if getting that new job causes me to have more responsibilities than I wish to take on?', 'What if improving at painting/dressmaking/car maintenance means that people will expect me to do things for them for free?'

Sometimes we sabotage because we feel we have reached an upper limit. Gay Hendricks, the psychologist and writer who first put forward the idea of the Upper Limit Problem, said it is as if we have an inner thermostat that monitors the amount of happiness, love and success we are allowed to experience. Once we cross the threshold of what we believe is acceptable for us, fear sets in and we sabotage in any way that works for us, to get ourselves back into the comfort zone. Do you believe there is a limit to how happy/successful/creative/loved you are allowed to be? Have you ever got close to that limit? If so, what did you do?

A client of mine, Alan, had a history of negative life events that meant he truly believed that if something went well, it was only a matter of time before something bad would happen. Part of our work together involved testing out new theories, e.g. the theory that highs do not always lead to lows, and people who are kind aren't always biding their time before they show you their true colours.

During one of these belief-testing periods, Alan came to a session and said, 'Aha, I knew it. Things were going too well. Then the other shoe dropped, didn't it!' I was all ears. What had happened? He told me that he had been having a period of success, and almost immediately the joy was ripped away from him in the form of an argument between him and his partner. I was sorry to hear this. He was clearly in distress. Once he felt more settled, we discussed the various possibilities for the argument they had. I was curious as to whether he really had found evidence that proved bad followed good, or whether confirmation bias had skewed his view of the world. As he talked, he admitted he might have started the argument as he had been so stressed that day. Stressed about what? Stressed that something was about to go wrong.

Life is unpredictable. Sometimes negativity comes out of the blue when all seems to have been going smoothly in life. However, Alan had not experienced that in this instant. He had been feeling as though things were going too well, and instead of enjoying the moment, he became fixated on the feeling that something bad would happen. So fixated that, he later admitted, he actively started looking for what could go wrong. His mind filled with potential but metaphorical boogeymen that could be lurking behind the next corner, causing so much stress that when he got home one evening, he snapped at his partner for the smallest thing. Instead of recognizing that he was the cause of the row that ensued, he saw the exchange of hurtful words and the sound of the slammed door as proof that he was right . . . Things really had been too good to be true.

Alan needed self-compassion to manage the distress he felt due to the incident and how cross he was with himself for missing what we found in the session. He needed to start a regular practice of putting his thoughts on trial, so he could see what he might be missing. And then, following this, he started to address his upper limit problem by creating a regular practice of celebrating his wins, taking mindful moments that helped him manage the emotional response caused by success and also gave him the ability to pause when he had the urge to 'reset his thermostat'. He also devised the following mantra: 'I am learning that I am allowed to feel good. There don't have to be limits to how long I can feel well or successful. I welcome in positivity.' Slowly and surely, he started to gather evidence that proved this mantra to be true.

Sometimes we fear success because it will change how others will see us – *If I succeed everyone will start talking about me/ will tear me down or shame me for doing well*. This can arise when success was not accepted and possibly shamed or undermined during childhood. I have worked with many people who saw family members being laughed at for trying and succeeding, or who were bullied for being 'swots' or 'nerds' by supposed friends when they were top of the class.

I have also worked with many people who struggle with success as they have grown up in countries, such as the UK, Australia and New Zealand, with tall poppy syndrome – the idea that no poppy should grow above the rest and when one tries, we must cut it down. Or in Scandinavian countries, where the Law of Jante – the tendency to disapprove of personal, individualistic success – is commonplace. When we grow up around those who say success is bad, it makes sense that we may procrastinate and act in ways that ensure failure to protect ourselves from the perceived threat of success.

Tall poppy syndrome is something many of us know well and have perhaps done to other people. Have you ever sneered about a friend or a celebrity when they have suddenly done well? 'Oh my god, have you seen her, she thinks she's so … (insert insult here) now that she has done this big thing', 'I bet she's self-obsessed', 'Well, I heard she's really unhappy', etc. On reflection, did you do this as their success triggered a fear that you were not as good in some way – a kind of envy – which led you to respond in a manner that made you feel more powerful?

I promise that you aren't alone if you recognize this response – the experience is so universal that British rock band The Smiths wrote a song called 'We Hate It When Our Friends Become Successful'. Other people's successes can seem like a mirror is being held up to us and make us feel insecure and like a failure, when this is rarely the case.

Growing up around envy and tall poppy syndrome can mean we learn to fear success, and even internalize envy – this is psychology speak that means we start to attack ourselves whenever we succeed at something, punishing ourselves the way other people might should we do something that could conceivably be coveted by others. It means we can start to sabotage ourselves when we get near success, undermining our talents, or we may not even try to succeed as we fear how others will treat us should we do well.

Unsticking points

- A more apt name for 'self-sabotage' is perhaps 'safety-seeking behaviour'. When viewed from this angle, you can see that the things you do to protect yourself may be better achieved another way.

- The secret to overcoming a fear is two-fold. The first part links to identifying and challenging the thoughts, fears and beliefs driving the behaviour (e.g. questioning whether you truly believe your fear thoughts). The second part involves challenging your thoughts and fears through experience (e.g. facing the fear over and over so that you learn you can survive it), or at least directly discussing what you fear so that others can support you to face your fears and show you they may or may not be as you expect.

Overcoming fear of success

Ask: what is my goal, and whose goal is it? If the goal is not yours, maybe you are getting in your own way as you really don't want that thing at all and part of you knows that. Maybe you keep procrastinating as you are going for a job your family wants you to have but you don't. Maybe you are going on dates but secretly don't want to date as you learned that this could end in arguments or tears. Return to the list of values in the previous chapter and align your next move with those instead.

If the goal really is one of your own, then ask: if I were to achieve this goal, what would that

---

mean for my life? What are the best things that could come from achieving this goal? What would be the worst things? What are the risks I will have to take to achieve this goal (e.g. putting myself out there, having other people notice me, potentially reject me, or even having other people abandon me after I succeed).

Once you have identified the experiences you might be protecting yourself from, ask: what other way could I support myself through the experience I fear? Could I speak to the people I fear will reject me? Can I lean on other friends? Can I use soothing skills to manage the anxiety I feel? Could I start a mantra practice, such as 'I am learning that I am allowed to be happy and successful'?

Help, I'm stuck

'I am going in circles when really, I should know better. I've always tended to be drawn to people who are cold and rejecting. Recently I met with three potential new agents and told myself that this time I was going to go for someone who will hold my hand a little. I needed someone warm and supportive. When I interviewed the agents, it was like when Goldilocks tried the three porridges: the first one was too direct and cold; the second so kind that in all honesty I felt uncomfortable; but the third seemed just

right – kind, calm and boundaried. I felt sure that number three was the exact middle ground I needed, so I went with them. But now, I am right back feeling like I picked someone cold and rejecting again. They were fully present in the first few weeks of our involvement while contracts were being signed but now I barely hear from them. I've done it again, I'm so annoyed with myself.'

—JORDAN, a fellow author who was looking for a literary agent (someone to represent his work, help hone his ideas, and connect him with publishers in order to get paid to write)

Jordan is not only a fellow author, he is also a fellow psychologist and an ex-supervisor of mine. When I was a trainee, I would rush to our supervision sessions with my client notes, a list of questions and star-gazey eyes that looked at him expectantly, waiting for him to share his wisdom with me. To me he knew it all and I hoped two things: that one day I would be as good a therapist as he, and that he would never know how many psychological flaws I felt I had. Back then I still believed that therapists had to have perfect mental health, and as they 'knew better', they would never make the kind of circular life choices I was so often wont to do. So, on the evening we finished working together, Jordan shared with me the above story of searching for the perfect literary agent and I was shocked. How could someone who knew so much about psychology still be repeating patterns? He shared this story with me on purpose. He knew I had him on a pedestal and that I thought that once people truly knew why they did something, and how to make different choices, they should simply stop doing that thing. And, well ... that just isn't the case.

Jordan's story is important because I know many people believe, as I did, that once they truly understand the patterns in their life, they will never repeat the patterns again. Who better to illustrate that this is definitely not the case than a person with an actual PhD in human psychology?

Jordan knew his history. He knew he had the tendency to push away people who could offer the warmth he now thought he wanted and needed. He had purposely tried to do something different but had found himself right back in the same old pattern. This wasn't because he didn't feel he deserved to be supported – if that had been the case, he would have gone with the first candidate. It also wasn't solely confirmation bias (i.e. interpreting the actions of others to fit your world view), as he had worked on this already. It was, in the main, because humans are drawn to what feels familiar.

He had turned down the second candidate, who could have offered him real warmth, as this level of kindness was unfamiliar to him and made him feel a little anxious. The third candidate offered what he wanted on paper and his 'gut' instinct about them was good. It felt like the perfect fit. Has this ever happened to you? Have you ever walked into an interview and there's something about the interviewer that reminds you of your sister, and suddenly everything feels a little easier? Have you ever decided to find a job, partner or community that was totally different to your usual preference and, six months in, found yourself feeling that somehow the new situation was almost exactly like the last? Even when we are equipped with the expert knowledge to overcome our sabotaging ways, we can still sometimes find ourselves in the same scenario. Being in situations that feel familiar often makes us feel relaxed, like we are already on the road to knowing the other person, place or thing. Your shoulders drop and you let your guard down.

Jordan recognized that familiarity had got him again, and after our chat quickly got his self-flagellation in check. He had two options. He could either leave his agent, call candidate number two and manage the unease their kindness gave him. Or he could stay and manage the relationship he already had in a different way, knowing that he could leave if nothing changed. He chose the latter option. He chose to write a list of the things he hoped for in their working relationship – weekly phone calls or email check-ins; feedback on his writing drafts that focused on what had been done well, not solely what needed changing; occasional coffee meetings where they could get to know each other more personally. He then shared this list with the agent, who was grateful for such clear guidance on how Jordan wished to be supported.

So many people believe that once they know about a pattern, it must never happen again, or they have failed. They believe it is proof that they can't be trusted not to self-sabotage. This is not the case. Remember what we learned at the end of Chapter 1? Patterns are hard to kick and lapsing into our old ways is normal. And the moment you notice you are back, doing something familiar, and choose to do something in a different way, like Jordan did, it is the opposite of sabotage, and a new and healthier pattern can ensue.

Unsticking points

- If you can't fully ditch a pattern, it is not because you are failing; it is because you are human.
- If you find yourself back in an old pattern, don't immediately assume you are stuck all over again. Remember you have options as to how to manage it. Decide whether you are going to leave or whether there is something you can do to make the situation better, such as communicating what you need or want within your familiar situations.

Chapter 4

Drama

Once upon a time, a really long time ago (sometime between 469 and 399 BC), the philosopher Socrates was walking the streets of Ancient Greece when someone he knew ran up to him and said, 'Do you know what I just heard about your student?' A clear invite into conversation, and, to the trained ear and eye, perhaps an offering of a little hot gossip too. Instead of taking the bait, however, Socrates replied that he wanted his acquaintance to pass the Triple Filter Test before he told him any more. The acquaintance acquiesced.

The first filter, Socrates told the man, was the filter of truth. So, Socrates asked him, 'Have you made absolutely sure that what you are about to tell me is true?' The man responded that he hadn't. It was a piece of information he had picked up quite recently, and was simply eager to share.

The second filter, Socrates said, was the filter of goodness. 'Is what you are about to tell me about my student something good?' he asked his acquaintance. The man, who I like to imagine was, at this point, starting to look flustered, said, 'No.' Apparently, and quite unsurprisingly to those of us who know how gossip works, he relayed that it was quite the opposite.

The third and final filter, Socrates said, was the filter of usefulness, and even though the man's information had not passed the previous two filters, Socrates told him that he still had this remaining chance. So, Socrates asked, 'Is what you want to tell me about my student going to be useful to me?' To which the acquaintance replied . . . it was not.

Reflecting on this, Socrates asked why – should the information not be true, good, or useful – the man should want to tell it to him at all? This concluded the conversation and reportedly left the man shamefaced.

The beginning of this story is one that most of us can relate to. The moment where a potentially tantalizing piece of information about someone we know is dangled in front of our noses. Each of us also likely knows the impact gossip can have, maybe because people have spread untruths or semi-truths about us in the past and we have felt the pain of it. Or because we have spread scandals without fact-checking and seen the devastated look on the faces of the people the gossip was about when they found out they were the topic on everyone's lips. The end of this story, where Socrates uses a system to judge whether the story should be told, however, and simply rejects the man's advance, is perhaps the more unrelatable aspect.

So far, we have looked at how people get stuck due to their habits, heuristics and the things they do to keep themselves safe. Now for the fourth reason . . . Sometimes we get stuck in life because we get drawn into drama in our relationships. Sometimes we take the place of Socrates and are invited into social games that could harm us and others by the people we know and love, and also by strangers too. Sometimes we take the role of the acquaintance, tempting others in. Whichever role we take on, however, as so few of us are truly aware of how pervasive drama is, and why it occurs, many of us don't even notice the repetitive interactions that we engage in that get in the way of our relationships and our goals. In line with that, this chapter will help you identify when and where you may get caught in drama, and how you can create your own version of the Triple Filter Test in order to get unstuck from these kinds of issues.

The drama triangle

Do you remember Little Red Riding Hood? Here's a quick refresher. As she crossed the forest on her way to her grandmother's house, she met a wolf who asked her where she was going. The wolf suggested she pick flowers for her grandmother, so that he could get to the house before her. When Red Riding Hood arrived, the wolf was already in bed wearing her grandmother's clothes, having gobbled her up. He then promptly did the same to Red Riding Hood. A short time later a woodsman entered the house. He cut open the now sleeping wolf, miraculously rescued the unscathed grandmother and Red Riding Hood, and then filled the somehow-still-sleeping wolf up with stones. When the wolf woke up, he tried to escape but the weight of the stones caused him to collapse and die.

The story follows a pattern that almost every cartoon and

fairy tale have in common. It has three roles: the victim (or, in this case, victims – Red Riding Hood and her grand-mother), the persecutor (the wolf) and the rescuer (the woodsman). You can also see this pattern in most action films, too. Think about *Die Hard*. The good guy, John McClane, comes home for Christmas to see his estranged wife and daughters. While he is at an office party, terrorists (the persecutors) enter, threatening the life of everyone in the building (the victims) and John finds that he is the only person who can save them all (the rescuer).

This script – known as the drama triangle, a behaviour model put forward by the American psychiatrist Stephen Karpman in the 1960s – plays out in almost all kinds of disa-greements, real or imaginary. Real life is usually a little more complex than goodies and baddies, but the point is, the script is everywhere.

Karpman believes that most interpersonal conflicts com-prise a rescuer, a persecutor and a victim. The obvious examples that come to mind include:

- the bullies (persecutor), the bullied (victim), and a helpful friend, teacher, boss or prosecutor (rescuer)
- the middle child (rescuer) who ends up mediating between the older and younger sibling (either of whom could be victim or persecutor)
- the fighting couple at the dinner table (victim and/ or persecutor) and the loving friend (rescuer) who tries to step in (*Why don't we all stop fighting and have a glass of wine?*)

It's basically Little Red Riding Hood, but usually without the murder and bloodshed.

Karpman posited that most conflicts revolve around these patterns of behaviour, and while we can take on any role at any time, depending on the argument we are engaged in, we tend to unconsciously gravitate towards one in particular. This might be due to the roles we saw others take on when we were younger, or we may have developed an affinity for this role as a response to our experiences in childhood. For example, people may be drawn to the rescuer role because they learned in childhood that they will receive the love and attention they need only when they offer to help. Therapists, like myself, are often rescuers.

None of this is problematic in itself, but we can find ourselves feeling stuck in life and in our relationships when these roles start to make us or others miserable. For example, the middle child may feel like they are constantly overlooked by the rest of the family, who demand the most attention; the couple may start to rely on their friends to placate them, always drawing others into their arguments.

Before we go any further into each of these roles and answer questions you probably have by now, such as what's the difference between rescuing and helping, and why you need to sit through the discomfort of having me tell you that from time to time you might have taken up the role of persecutor ... we need a caveat. In this chapter we are going to learn that there are moments where we put ourselves in the 'victim' role. These are the moments where we become the victim because we discount our skills, abilities and options. These are not the moments where others really are harming or oppressing us, making us the victim. That is a very different thing. This chapter is not a victim-blaming exercise. If you have experienced abuse of any kind, you deserve compassion and support to manage what you have been through. You are not to blame.

I avoided the drama triangle model for a long time. I felt outraged when I first learned about it, as my line of work involves supporting people who have had terrible atrocities committed against them, such as physical and sexual abuse, people who have not been listened to or believed and who have had others ask, 'Well, what did you do in order for that to happen?' Victim blaming is unacceptable, and as I thought this model was set up to do just that, I rejected it for a long time. In addition to this, I have never seen someone feel empowered to make change through being told that they are 'playing the victim' or that they have a 'victim's mindset'. I simply couldn't see how this model would be useful.

I only came back to the drama triangle once I rethought the model and realized two things: 1) when it comes to abuse, this model helps us understand how an aggressor might put someone and keep someone in the victim role, which is different to the times when we choose to put ourselves in this role; and 2) when it comes to life in general, this model helps us to understand our role in the repetitive conflicts in our lives, such as the fights we get into over the washing-up, or the times we think people aren't listening to us, or when we burn out from offering too much of our time and care. Or when, no matter how hard we try, we feel like we are reliving the same drama over and over again. A core reason people feel stuck is because of the interactions in their relationships, so, I had to admit, this model had its uses, and that's why I am now sharing it with you.

Going forward, when I use the term 'victim' in this chapter, please be mindful that, unless otherwise stated, I am not referring to people who have been attacked or persecuted in any way. This is simply a useful model to be aware of when it comes to patterns of behaviour and conflict, and if you need further support, please don't hesitate to seek it out. You will find useful resources to point you in the right direction at the end of this book.

Unsticking points

- We can get stuck in life when, during conflict, we don't tackle the situation at hand effectively but instead take up roles that create drama.
- The drama triangle doesn't solely play out between individuals; it arises between communities, countries and strangers across history, time and time again.
- We tend to gravitate towards one role in our lives. If a role is important or feels natural to us, we may find situations in which we can play that role in an ongoing way (e.g. rescuers may become therapists, or may partner with people who they believe need a lot of support).
- We usually take on the role without conscious awareness.

The roles we play

The drama triangle looks like this:

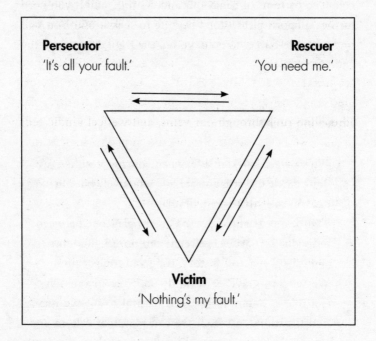

Persecutor
'It's all your fault.'

Rescuer
'You need me.'

Victim
'Nothing's my fault.'

The Persecutor

No one ever wants to imagine themselves as a persecutor, but we've all been guilty of it from time to time. So, try not to squirm away from it and open your mind to times you may have been overly nitpicky or passive-aggressive or even all-out aggressive.

When we're in the role of the persecutor, we act like a

strict and critical parent, blaming, criticizing and finding fault in others around us. We need to 'win' no matter what the cost, so we may point out all the reasons the other person is wrong and refuse to back down in an argument or discussion. We may use blaming statements in order to control people around us, such as: 'It's my way or the highway' or 'I knew I should never have trusted you' or 'If you had done exactly what I said it wouldn't have gone wrong'. We may act in ways that subtly control the people around us, or, more obviously, we may bully people. When in this role, adrenaline runs through our veins, and we feel vindicated, because we believe we are right. When people suggest that our behaviour is unkind or that we are incorrect, we may either be totally shocked, or we may become defensive, rushing off all the reasons we are justified in our critical and controlling demeanour.

People who are regularly drawn to the persecutor role may seem dominant and strong, but they behave like this for multiple reasons. They may have witnessed others acting in this way when they were younger and now subconsciously copy their behaviour, or perhaps they are trying to hide their own vulnerability. Maybe they felt like the victim for a long time and being the persecutor helps to avoid feelings of failure or chaos, or a lack of recognition, or a fear of being seen as a victim themselves. Sometimes, people who tend towards the persecutor role at more extreme levels have a background of abuse or trauma.

We can recognize that we are in this role when we feel superior, discount another person's worth or ability, or when we start blaming or wanting to control the actions of others.

The Rescuer

When we are in the rescuer role, we strive to help others. This isn't when we are being helpful in an empowering way, supporting others to create a long-term solution. People in the rescuer role offer others a quick fix to their problem and maybe say things like: 'Don't worry, I am here to fix it' or 'Don't worry, it's all going to be fine'. Most people think this is the best role in the drama triangle, but each of the roles comes with its own pitfalls.

The temporary relief the rescuer provides isn't helpful in the long run. By stepping in and doing everything for someone else, the rescuer can set up a cycle of dependency, making the other person the victim who needs saving rather than another adult who, with the right support, could do these tasks for themselves. You're probably familiar with the expression, 'If you give a man a fish, you feed him for a day. If you teach a man to fish, you feed him for a lifetime.' When we rescue others without thinking about what the other person truly needs, we give them a fish for a day but never allow them to develop the skills to stand on their own two feet.

Rescuers often see persecutors as people who want to control every situation without realizing that they are doing the same thing. They, too, often want to step in to manage someone else's emotional distress because they believe they have all the answers. Even though their intentions are good, being a rescuer inadvertently makes the other person the victim. Rescuers can also alienate the people around them, by always trying to step in and fix a situation when the other person doesn't want to be fixed, but instead wants to be heard.

We can also 'rescue' ourselves by providing quick fixes rather than long-term solutions. We rescue ourselves when we reach for a glass of wine at the end of a hard day, or dive into a Netflix binge or endless Instagram scroll. We immediately reduce our stress in the moment, but these methods do nothing to get to the bottom of the issue we are experiencing. If you remember our discussion in Chapter 1, it is often these moments of self-rescuing that turn into our personal bad habits.

People who are drawn to the rescuer role may have learned the role from the people they grew up with, or they saw that helping others got them the attention or support they needed. Perhaps they were a carer at a young age because a parent died or was unwell and they had to step into a responsible position earlier than was developmentally appropriate. Sometimes we become rescuers simply because seeing other people in distress makes us feel anxious, so we do everything in our power to fix their situation, as rectifying their emotional state feels more manageable than facing and dealing with our own discomfort. Rescuers often feel guilty when they don't step in to help. If this is you, don't forget that wanting to help others is a good thing! But people drawn to this role may notice that their sense of wellbeing relies on helping others, or that focusing on the needs of others creates a welcome distraction from their own problems and so they don't help themselves.

The Victim

When we are in the victim role, we tend to feel like the world is against us. Remember, I am not talking about the obvious moments of victimization such as bullying, harassment or worse. I am also not talking about trauma responses, in which you start truly believing that the world is a dangerous place because you have had the experience that people cannot be trusted. I am talking about our day-to-day experiences, such as when no one responds to our message on the group chat and we assume it's because everyone is annoyed with us. Or when we blame others for all our misfortune, without considering the agency we have in our lives. I am talking about the moments where we are not actually powerless, but where we disempower ourselves by forgetting about our own resources and ability to take charge in our lives.

The person in the victim role will undermine themself and discount their abilities. They will feel powerless, like they can't problem-solve and have no options. Victims in this sense don't look at their own responsibility, instead blaming everything on the persecutor, while waiting for the rescuer to come and save them. If we're in the victim role, we tend to have unrealistic expectations, thinking that if others cared enough, they would help us, and assume that other people will inherently know what we need even when we haven't told them. If we are in victim mode, we may forget that there are actions we can take to manage or overcome whatever issue we are facing, and if a rescuer doesn't come, we may interpret this as further proof that our situation is hopeless.

Can you see how these roles could make us feel stuck? Something happens that causes us discomfort, and instead of working through the unease and coming to a conclusion that works for everyone, or instead of taking responsibility for ourselves, we slip into a role that makes us go in circles and we invite other people to take up other roles that keep the drama alive.

It's important to know that we don't always choose our role. Have you ever been made to feel like you were incapable of doing anything without someone else's help? Maybe a boss micromanaged you to the point of you starting to question your own ability, or a friend was so critical of you that you automatically felt on edge the moment you saw them. If these scenarios are familiar to you, the role you have been put in was not your choice. It's what happens after we are put into this position that matters.

If we start believing that we do not have options, we feel stuck because we have fallen into the drama triangle trap. If, however, we recognize that there are actions we could take – such as seeking support from a colleague who can share the emotional burden of the micromanaging boss, reminding ourselves of our actual abilities, or creating boundaries with our critical friend – we are not falling into the victim role.

If we return to the example at the beginning of the chapter, can you now see what was happening? The acquaintance wanted to be seen as the helpful rescuer, handing the esteemed Socrates vital information. Really, the man was in the role of the persecutor, delighting in the criticism and shame he was about to share. He wanted to bring Socrates into his drama, and into the persecutor role alongside him, but Socrates said no. Instead of stepping onto the drama triangle, he refused the role that he was offered, and you can too!

Unsticking points

- Learning that you tend towards one role is not a moment to shame yourself. That role will have offered you protection at some point in your life, but it has now stopped being so helpful. Be compassionate with yourself.
- Recognizing the times we have been put into a role that we didn't choose is imperative so that we can know what we need to do to get out of that role. You can consider your options and, assuming we are not talking about a situation in which you are in physical danger, decide to address the issues at hand.

Getting aware of your role in the drama triangle

Repeat after me: *I am willing to consider that I may adopt these roles from time to time. I am willing to consider how they may affect my relationships and my health. I am committed to creating change for the sake of the people around me, and myself as well.* This is important as the first step to overcoming the drama triangle involves being willing to acknowledge that we may engage in these patterns and that we can take responsibility for our actions.

Reflect across your life and ask yourself if there is a role that stands out to you. Which do you tend

---

towards the most? Consider why it would be helpful to know this answer. Will it help your relationships? Your work? Will it help empower you?

The three faces of victimhood

The day I first sat down to write this chapter, I witnessed myself within the space of one hour move seamlessly between playing the persecutor in an argument with my partner, the rescuer in a chat with my upset friend, and the victim on a call with an ex-micromanaging boss. We really can take up any role at any time – and without warning, too. But this is only the beginning of it. The next thing we need to know is that we can switch roles any time during the same conflict ...

Help, I'm stuck

'I do so much for other people in my life, and no one ever asks how I am. They often just take the support and never learn or change their behaviour. I really need a break, but if I stop doing everything, nothing will get done. I am annoyed and feel so alone.'

—CHARLIE, 56

Charlie came to therapy feeling tired. She had always been the shoulder to cry on, the person everyone turned to, the one at work who knew everyone's birthdays and exactly what they were hoping for as a gift this year. She had read enough Instagram posts and self-help books to know she was a people-pleaser, but she couldn't understand why she was so angry with the people around her right now. She felt like there was no way out of her situation. She didn't recognize herself in this tense role. She usually had such a sunny demeanour and derived great joy from her social network. It had been her birthday a week prior and two of her friends hadn't texted to wish her well and she took this as a sign that people were starting to avoid her – possibly, she worried, because her behaviour was erratic.

The pattern that was causing her to feel stuck arose almost immediately in our first conversation, when she described a fight she had had with her son, Max, who had been ill recently. She initially described how her 'poorly boy' (her words) had needed her there, but then he had kept asking for things and she had finally lost it. My initial impression was of a boy under ten, and a mum stretched to the limits reaching the end of her tether. Then she mentioned storming out of his house, and I was confused.

I was right about her being stretched to her limits. However, her son was twenty-five and had moved out four years earlier to a house in the neighbouring town. He was not a child but a man studying for a masters in physics, who lived on his own and had a membership to the local rock-climbing centre. Once we got this sorted, we started the conversation again.

Six weeks prior to our conversation, Max had reportedly

been unwell with a bad cold and, 'as she always did', Charlie had been helping him. She said she called the doctors on his behalf. She went to the supermarket to fill his cupboards – which she did weekly anyway, but thought she would do it again. She did his laundry and tidied his house while he slept. When he woke up, instead of thanking her, he asked her to go out and get something else from the shop. She snapped. 'Of course, it doesn't matter that Mummy is run ragged or has other stuff to do, no one ever cares about her . . .' Max was shocked, but she carried on, saying he needed to get a grip and look after himself. He started to defend himself, but she was so angry that she shouted, 'Next time you feel unwell, don't bother calling me. You need to grow up; it's pathetic that you still need me to do everything.' This was when she stormed out.

A few days later she called him to make amends. He sounded upset. He said he had little food in the house, and that since she had walked out, he had been hungry. She felt terrible. Why had she got so angry? Why had she stormed out? Now her son was hungry, and it was her fault. She cancelled her appointments and rushed to the supermarket for more supplies.

This was a snapshot of what was happening in many areas of Charlie's life, and it was causing her to act in ways she could not understand. The drama triangle had got her in a trap, with Charlie stuck as the rescuer and Max the victim. This was understandable. As a child, Max had been very unwell and so Charlie had to be there for him all the time. Max had grown up, but the pattern was ongoing. It was as if they were still stuck in their earliest roles, possibly explaining my feeling that she must have been talking about a very young child. Charlie was a kind mum, but by giving and giving until she couldn't give anymore, she had become resentful. She felt taken advantage of and had slipped from being the rescuer to the victim.

This is a learning point for all of us. Whichever role you begin with in the drama triangle, if you play it for long enough you will always end up feeling like you are the victim. This is why the drama triangle is also known as 'the three faces of victimhood'. The rescuer gets annoyed that their efforts aren't being recognized and the persecutor gets annoyed that others aren't following their guidance. Can you think of a time this has happened to you? Maybe you criticize your partner for never tidying up (persecutor) but you feel hurt because you are always cleaning the house (victim). Or maybe you're the one who never tidies up (persecutor) and when your partner snaps at you, instead of taking responsibility (which would be the way out of the drama triangle), you feel like the victim as you were snapped at.

After discussing the drama triangle and the different roles she was playing, Charlie started to realize that, although she had the best intentions, continuously helping Max discounted his abilities as an adult. She never gave him the opportunity to learn how to look after himself, so the cycle couldn't end. She had even slipped into the persecutor role when she called him 'pathetic'. When she got in touch with him after the fight, instead of having a conversation and addressing the balance in their relationship, they immediately resumed their roles: son as victim, mum as rescuer.

When we engage in the drama triangle often, we will always find a way to reset to our most comfortable roles. Max wasn't being intentionally manipulative, but after years of being supported in this way, he had learned not to trust his own abilities. Being in their roles served them both well, as it kept their relationship extremely close: Charlie felt needed, and Max felt nurtured. But now, they needed to find an expression of love and care that didn't lead to resentment and allowed Max to stand on his own two feet. To break the cycle, they both needed to recognize their roles, without judgement, and work together to strengthen their beliefs in each other. This was a slow and steady journey, but it improved their relationship tenfold.

Unsticking points

- No matter which role we take, we (usually) end up feeling like the victim.
- Learning to address issues of imbalance in relationships and set boundaries before we become resentful is imperative, as is recognizing our responsibility in the dramas we play.

Can you see the times you switched roles?

- **Think of a recent argument/conflict you had with a relative, friend or colleague.** Write down the people involved. Was it two or more of you? Starting at the beginning, which role did each person in the conflict play? Were you the one

---

correcting the other person (in which case you could be the persecutor or the rescuer) or was the other person (people) doing this to you (in which case you would have been the 'victim')? What happened next? And how did you end up feeling? Did you leave feeling like a victim? Or something else? What belief about that person, yourself or the world did it confirm?

- **Think of a repetitive conflict in a relationship of yours.** Do the same exercise as you just completed. Is there a pattern? Have you been taking on specific roles and then switching to the victim at a certain point, or have you addressed the heart of the issue? If you are like the middle child we discussed earlier, the one who feels overlooked, have you been in the rescuer role for so long that others are now used to it, and you now feel like the victim who has no way to be seen by the people you care about? Did you then tell your family how you felt and ask for more care, or did you switch into persecutor mode and start criticizing them instead? If you are part of the couple who always rely on the friend to mediate, and suddenly they say enough is enough, did you feel like they had let you down and clearly didn't care about you enough to help out? If so, did you find another way to face the issues in the relationship, or did you start criticizing the friend? If you have a demanding colleague whose constant requests are making you anxious, did you set a boundary with them, stating what you could and couldn't do within your allotted time, or did you start moaning about what a terrible person they are to the other people in your team? No one will see your answers, so be as honest with yourself as you can. Once you have identified the pattern, decide what you could do to get out of the victim role going forward. If you are unsure how to do this, read to the end of the chapter and return to this exercise then.

The games we play without meaning to

Learning to recognize what role you are playing, and whether you have put yourself there by choice or not, are the first steps to getting out of the drama triangle. To fully break the cycle, however, we need to know a little about what blinds us to the situation we find ourselves in.

Once we've been caught in the drama triangle for a while, we sometimes start to play games, with very specific patterns and predictable outcomes that, most of the time, ensure we stay in our favourite role and get an outcome we (unconsciously) crave. We rarely recognize we are playing these games, nor would we choose to play them if we were fully aware of our motives and behaviours. These games help us to create and replay drama in our lives, further keeping us stuck.

Games aren't played for fun, but to meet a need that we either aren't explicitly aware of or that we feel would be unacceptable to another person, if we had simply asked. When the Canadian psychiatrist Eric Berne put forward the idea of games in his book *Games People Play*, he gave a simple example that I think we can all understand: if you have children or know any young siblings, you may have noticed that when one is sick, the other suddenly says 'me too', when you know they are perfectly well. This is an example of a game. The young child (let's call him Jimmy) wants the same attentive care as their unwell sibling. They engage in this game either because they know they would be scolded if they said, 'It's not fair! I want to be treated like that too!' when their sibling is genuinely unwell, or they engage in this as they don't know what exactly they want, but they are driven to pursue it regardless.

Whatever games we play, we tend to do it because we:

1. don't want (or know how) to communicate what we want

2. crave someone's attention but don't want to ask for it

3. want to create a sense of intimacy without having to say we want to be close to that person, as so many of us believe asking for intimacy will make us look needy

4. want to avoid things that make us feel uncomfortable

5. are subconsciously reenacting old scripts

6. are looking for a way to pass the time – playing games can make us feel powerful, needed, or simply divert us

7. are repeating what we saw when we were young

You might read this list and wonder why we persist with playing games when they don't make us any happier. Sometimes negative interactions are more bearable than having no interaction from the people we care about, and as you know, repeated actions with known outcomes make us feel calm, even when that outcome is negative. Plus, most of us don't feel able to either ask for what we want, or know what we want in the first place – meaning we don't even know a game is being played!

Not all games are harmful, but when played often enough, they can get us stuck by entrenching unhelpful beliefs, ensuring needs don't get met and creating frustrations in relationships. Let's go back to our friend Jimmy, who said he was sick too. This kind of game does no harm and is usually recognized by the adults involved as an expression of desire for care and they respond accordingly. When not understood, however, an innocuous game like this may repeat often enough that the child may start to believe that to get care one must be ill, which is a very dangerous cycle.

The classics

To help you get a sense of the games you may have found yourself engaged in before, here are a couple of classics (others will be discussed throughout the rest of the chapter):

Game 1: 'Why don't you . . . ? Yeah, but . . .'

Have you ever told a friend about a struggle you're having – maybe something happened at work, or you've had an argument with a friend – and they stepped in to solve it for you? Instead of listening and sympathizing, they ask: 'Why don't you [insert suggestion here]?', to which you respond: 'I could try that, but [and you then list the myriad of reasons why this suggestion would not work]'. Your friend then says: 'I know, why don't you . . .', and you reply: 'Yeah, I mean, I could, but . . .' and this goes on until you both feel deeply frustrated. You feel misunderstood and angry that your friend didn't intuit what you needed, and that your inability to find a solution was proof that your predicament really was as terrible as you thought it might be ('I knew it, I can't be helped'). And your friend feels confused or frustrated, as nothing they suggest seems to work.

If so, you already know what I'm talking about. When we find ourselves in this situation, it is either because we are unaware that we simply want our friend to say, 'Wow, that's hard, I am so sorry,' or it can be because we believe we are not allowed to ask for support or sympathy, lest we come across a victim. So, we play a covert game in the hopes our friend will read our mind and connect with us, but it ultimately compounds our initial position of feeling like our situation is hopeless.

The game is not always initiated by the person with the problem, however. Sometimes we share how we feel with a friend, and it triggers their inner rescuer, and they start trying to rescue us when they weren't asked to. If we recognize what is happening and say, 'I was actually just wanting to share how I feel, I am not ready for solutions yet,' then the game doesn't take on a life of its own. If, however, you notice you start saying why each suggested solution won't work, you are in the game. You just didn't initiate it.

We are drawn to people who offer us an opportunity to take up our favourite role. And we are drawn to people who are willing to play certain games. For example, people who play 'Why don't you . . . ? Yeah, but . . .' will often find people who love to play the game 'I was only trying to help', which is the moment when the person who has taken on the rescuer role feels resentful or frustrated and switches from the rescuer to the victim role.

This game doesn't only arise around emotional struggles. It could happen in any situation, such as if you show someone your work and they start rushing in with suggestions about how to change it, or if you picked up this book and everything you read made you think, 'Yeah, but that wouldn't work for me because . . .' If this is the case, ask yourself whether it really is true that the suggestions wouldn't work, or whether you are looking for something else instead – like a calm, reassuring voice saying to you, 'You know what, life sucks sometimes.' If that's what you are looking for, consider it said! I hope you get some rest and are treated with kindness by the people in your life.

Game 2: Blemish

Have you ever felt envious of or upset with someone else and, rather than admit that to yourself, found fault in the other person? This is the blemish game. It arises when we feel 'less than' or insecure in some way, and to manage it and feel more powerful, we unconsciously become the persecutor and start to look for their blemishes. Tall poppy syndrome, which we discussed in the last chapter, is a good example of the blemish game played at an international scale.

Focusing on blemishes can be a way to avoid how we truly feel and can also be a way of bonding with others. So far we have only talked about gossip in a negative light, but, if you are totally honest, how many times have you bad-mouthed someone with others and felt a sense of connection as they nodded along, as well as a little superior to the person you are gossiping about?

The blemish game doesn't just create rifts between people and keep our true feelings away from ourselves, it is a game that can keep generations of people stuck and alienated from each other. For example, when some people get older, they start to feel insecure about the younger generation – maybe as they believe the younger generation see them as irrelevant – so a game of blemish ensues ('Well, no wonder millennials can't afford housing, they spend all their money on avocados and fancy coffee!'). It works both ways, with younger generations saying, 'Boomers talk about our finances, but they're the ones that got the pensions that we will never get.' Every older generation thinks the younger one is work-shy or has it easy, and every younger generation thinks the older generation is stuck in the mud. This game of continuously proving who's on top stops us from learning from each other, and often it is a charade that covers up the insidious effects of ageism and the fear of being judged.

'Blemish' also keeps us from taking responsibility for actions that cause us to feel shame. For example, if someone tells you that you did something wrong and it makes you feel defensive and unacceptably vulnerable, you may find yourself saying, 'Well, it's not like you're an angel,' before going on to list all their imperfections that have just sprung to mind that have nothing to do with this scenario. 'Blemish' may protect us from painful feelings in the short term, but it impedes resolution, personal growth and human connection.

Unsticking points

- When we play the same games, they keep unhelpful beliefs and stories we tell ourselves alive (i.e. 'others can't help'; 'others aren't as smart as me').
- Games create short-term feel-good moments but ultimately get in the way of our relationships and our ability to ask for or recognize what we need.
- You can step out of a game by naming what is happening or what you would like to happen instead. You can choose instead to have a direct conversation with your friend or walk away until you feel calm.

The blame game

A big reason so many of us are stuck in the drama triangle is because heuristics and many of the games we play make other people the problem, meaning we often can't see our part.

Have you heard of fundamental attribution error? It's the tendency to attribute our actions to our situation and context, instead of our character, and vice versa for other people. For example, if we are late for work, we may say it's due to bad traffic, but if others are late to meet us, we assume they are being disrespectful. This means that we are more likely to give ourselves a break than we are to give other people a break. This is another way the media hooks us in, printing stories about mistakes people make, as if this is a sign that person is a true moron. The media loves the drama triangle and games, and so, when we consume it, we need to be aware of the one-sidedness of articles, as we discussed in Chapter 2, and also of the ways the media positions the protagonists of their stories.

Whenever we notice we are being dragged into believing another person is 'bad', we need to consider: 1) am I playing a game of blemish because I am feeling insecure, angry, or less than in some way? and 2) am I making assumptions about them that I would not make about myself?

We must give other people the same benefit of the doubt that we give ourselves. For this, I find Hanlon's razor particularly helpful: 'Never attribute to malice that which is adequately explained by stupidity.' In other words, many of the 'bad behaviours' we see are, in reality, unintentional mistakes. For the sake of balance, however, this does not mean that you should blindly assume everyone is doing their best.

Fundamental attribution error is a bias like those we learned about in Chapter 2, rather than a game. There are, however, games that cause us to blame others in a similar way.

Games 3 and 4: 'Look what you made me do' and 'If it weren't for you . . .'

Do you remember Sam, who was trying to stop drinking in Chapter 1? Sam didn't just have to remove the cues triggering her drinking and come up with other, healthier options, as described in Chapter 1. She had to contend with two games that kept her stuck. Firstly, during our conversations, Sam recounted several times when friends had annoyed her, and she used that as an excuse to drink: *Look what you made me do*. This made us realize that she hadn't kept her plan to stop drinking a secret purely as a means to keep her privacy, as she had said in our initial meetings. She had found that not telling them created an opportunity for another game that helped her in the short term: it meant she could tell people that she couldn't stop drinking until her housemates stopped drinking too – *If it weren't for them, I would have already quit*. These games are extremely common, and both mean we get to shift the responsibility of our behaviour onto others. In Sam's case, it meant she didn't have to admit that she really just wanted a drink.

Sam successfully became sober, after taking responsibility for her actions and doubling down on the steps we discussed in Chapter 1, but she noticed these games followed her into her new life.

One day, while begrudgingly writing urgent notes for a three-hour Zoom meeting that she'd just completed, her partner bustled into her office. At the same time as her partner's smiling face emerged through the door, she accidentally deleted the paragraph she had just typed. She snapped, 'Look what you made me do!', and her confused and upset partner, who had just wanted to ask what she wanted to eat that evening, left the room. After Sam's irritation passed, she remembered she had shouted that all too familiar statement and started to wonder whether she was genuinely annoyed by the intrusion or if this was another version of a game she used to play. Her theory: she hadn't yet learned how to set boundaries around her time and space. So, instead of telling her partner that she needed an hour to concentrate, she blamed him for the error she had made so he would go away.

A month later, Sam completed the values activity from Chapter 2 and was really excited about getting into her new value-driven life – she was going to apply for a new job, learn a new language and spend a weekend away in a different country – but soon her partner was in the bad books again. 'He doesn't want to do those things, so I can't do them either.' She could do each of these activities alone, so why did her partner's choice mean she couldn't do them? We both recognized the familiar scent of the blame game – *If it weren't for you . . .*

'If it weren't for you/them . . .' is a game we usually play when we are (unconsciously or otherwise) afraid to do something we say we are going to do. In Sam's case, she wanted to put herself out there . . . in theory. But she was terrified of trying the new things. What if she failed? Sam was blaming her partner as a way to keep things the same; she just wasn't aware of it. After realizing how this game protected her from her fears, how it was a sneaky form of self-sabotage, we made a plan of action that mapped onto the steps I gave you in Chapter 2, i.e. recognize the fear, put the fear on trial, follow the 'what ifs' to the end, set up a behavioural experiment that tests out your theories and gently introduce yourself to the feared situation, building up your courage bit by bit. See Appendix 3 for a step-by-step on how you can follow this plan too.

So many of us play these games without awareness. What makes them particularly hard to recognize is that there are times where it really is the case that other people or circumstances hold us back. Perhaps you're a new parent and need additional support in order to begin a new hobby, or maybe you are in a controlling relationship where the other person will not allow you to make independent choices – and so, learning to get clear on where the barriers are in our head and in the real world is an important practice for each of us.

These blame games don't just keep us stuck and distracted from our responsibility in the drama around us, meaning we stay stuck in the victim role in the ways described here; they reinforce certain beliefs, like 'things will never change' or 'relationships hold me back'. And they reinforce our belief that we are passive and blameless, and that change is needed only from those around us. For example, sometimes when we don't want to make a decision for ourselves, we may let others do it for us – then, if the decision was bad, we don't have to take responsibility for the outcome; we can say, 'Look what you made me do!' On these occasions, we set up an opportunity to play the blame game and put the other person in the persecutor role.

Unsticking points

- Games will make us believe that other people are to blame, meaning we don't recognize how we contribute to our own feelings of stuckness.
- 'Look what you made me do' and 'If it weren't for you ...' are two examples of this. These games are often played at subtle levels in our day-to-day lives. At the most extreme end, they can be employed by abusers to keep their victims oppressed (e.g. when an abuser blames the person they attacked on the grounds that they were 'too annoying').
- If you are unsure who is responsible, use the suggestion from Chapter 3, and start with the assumption that it could be 50/50 – 50 per cent your responsibility and 50 per cent someone or something else's, and then look for the evidence that supports that.

Are games keeping you stuck?

- **Think about a time where you played one of the games above.** When did it happen? Why did it happen? If nothing comes to mind, think about a time where you felt sad, confused, misunderstood or rageful recently ... Did you play one of those games then? Did you meet someone fantastic but, instead of getting to know them or addressing the

---

insecurities you felt being in their presence, you told everyone they seemed arrogant and destroyed the chance of a relationship with them? Do you maintain your sense of feeling useful through helping out everyone around you, and instead of conceding that they may want a different kind of support, snap, 'I'm only trying to help' when they don't take your advice? Do you unintentionally create incidents or blame people for mishaps that will make them (other people) go away, rather than tell them you need space?

- **Return to the list of actions you are wanting to turn into habits and ask yourself if any games are getting in the way of you starting them.** Have you been saying you can't start until other people are on board, when actually you could do it – if slightly differently – alone? Have you told people you desperately want to start a new activity and found that every time they offer solutions you generate a thousand reasons why they are wrong? If so, could it be that you are playing 'If it weren't for you . . .' or 'Why don't you . . . ? Yeah, but . . .', and what you really need is to find ways to manage your fears of doing something alone, or to tell someone you care about that you are having a hard time at the moment and could really do with some emotional support? If you identify a game, consider what is causing the game and what you might do instead in order to put your new habits into action. If you are unsure what may lie beneath the game, don't worry; the next section will help you address that.

One game, multiple reasons

You now have a good handle on the drama triangle and some of the most common games. The next step is to get savvy about the drivers that cause you to play your personal games. This is where it can get a bit tricky.

Game 5: 'Now I've got you, you son of a bitch'

At one point I had five clients in my clinic who were playing the exact same game – a game no one likes to admit that they play, but we all do, and for various reasons.

At its heart, 'Now I've got you, you son of a bitch' involves one person backing another into a metaphorical corner, and then leaping with delight when they react. A quick note: if someone starts this game with you, the only way to not play is to walk away.

Have you ever met someone who will poke at the people around them, trying to start an argument? My first client was this person. He came to therapy because others repeatedly told him he had anger issues. He did not agree; he thought he was just having a laugh. Whenever he was at a social event and people were discussing a big topic, he would drop something controversial like 'Sexism is made up' or '5G will give you brain cancer' into conversation. If no one said anything, he would say something more controversial, speak a little louder, cite research articles he had read, and so on, until someone bit, taking him to task on his comments. The moment they did, he was elated (*Now I've got you!*). He had won.

He said he did it for fun. However, when we really got into it, it became clear he had always worried that others thought they were smarter than him and he feared being ignored, so he found a way that seemed to meet both these needs. He truly wanted connection and recognition but didn't feel he could ask for it, so he played this game to get people to listen. Goading people into paying him attention unfortunately left them not wanting to talk to him and thinking he wasn't smart at all, as his arguing tactics involved intimidation and shouting rather than listening and debating – confirming his worst fears, as so many of our behaviours do.

My second client wanted help with her marriage. She was so angry at her husband. Everything he did was annoying. She would ask him to sort the bills or the laundry, but he never did the job properly, or at least not as well as she did it. When they were socializing, he didn't host in the attentive way she liked, and she found it impossible not to tell him what he had done wrong. She noticed that a lot of their relationship involved him not doing things quite right and her telling him so. We could both agree that these instances sounded irritating but even Jane admitted she felt more rage than necessary for each of these minor misdemeanours.

After a lot of digging, it transpired that Jane's husband had an affair a few years back. They had decided to stay together, and Jane felt that she could forgive and forget. However, as you can imagine, that was easier said than done. She was still livid about his affair but didn't feel able to express her anger. And so, the rage bubbled away. Jane was subconsciously waiting for him to slip up so that the moment he set a foot wrong, her anger would overflow into 'Now I've got you' moments.

My next clients were a married couple who wanted to communicate better to improve their relationship, which felt stuck. One of the instances that played out in the therapy room involved the husband asking his wife if she was okay. The wife said she was fine, but moments later the husband asked, 'Are you okay?' The wife, again, said yes. There was silence. The husband then said, 'You're not okay, are you? I can tell!', and the wife's eyes opened wider in frustration: 'I've just said I'm okay, haven't I?' The husband then pounced: 'I knew it, you are angry with me, and you don't feel you can tell me.' He was afraid his wife was angry with him but didn't feel he could ask, and the game he played left him feeling vindicated and both of them feeling frustrated and unable to move forward in their relationship.

My final client was very progressive and always tried to be on top of whatever new lesson or hot take there was around social injustice. She took it upon herself to be informed but also to sniff out the people who weren't 'woke' enough and 'needed educating'. She would start talking to people about current affairs and would keep throwing out stats that she had learned that day, until the other person said that they didn't already know that information. When this happened, she would be shocked, and would shame them for not knowing everything she did. She genuinely believed she was being a good person by doing this. Unfortunately, the conversations weren't helping anyone at all, but if someone had pointed this out to her at the time she would have been affronted. In this instance, 'Now I've got you, you son of a bitch' was a cover for her fear she wasn't doing enough, and so she played this game until she could prove that she was indeed more virtuous and doing better than others.

These are all very different variations of the same game, and they all require very different solutions – the first client needed support with his relationships and self-worth, the second needed space to truly recover from the impact of the affair, the third pair needed to work on effective communication, and the final client, once she realized the game she had been playing and why, found she didn't need any further support, as simply acknowledging her rescuer tendencies helped her let go of this pattern.

If we want to get out of our negative patterns and game playing, we must get savvy to our wants, needs and what may be lurking underneath our surface behaviours. When you notice you end up in conflict, what do you really need? Is it that you are really standing your ground for an annoyance of yours? Or are you wanting someone to change a behaviour you don't like? Is it that there is something about them that makes you feel uncomfortable, i.e. they make you feel weak or less than, or they seem like a victim, and you can't handle that? Identify what is underneath and address that thing.

Some games have common drivers that can help you consider what might drive your own games: we often start 'Why don't you ...? Yeah, but ...' and 'If it weren't for you ...' in order to gain reassurance for something; we often play 'Look what you made me do' and 'If it weren't for you ...' and 'I'm only trying to help' to get rid of feelings of guilt, blame or suspicion; and finally, we often play the blemish game and 'Now I've got you, you son of a bitch' to feel powerful, in control, or to vent repressed feelings of anger.

If this doesn't clear up what is driving you, consider this: most games have themes of power, love and care. So, when you play a game, ask yourself whether you feel powerless in some way. If so, why? If you feel unloved in some way; if so, why? If you are angry for some reason; if so, why? Free-writing everything that comes up linked to the situation you were in can help identify underlying feelings, as can keeping a journal over time, which shows you if any patterns arise in what gets you going in an argument. Once you identify what you might be feeling and need, decide how you will address those things. Also, a quick note: some people simply play these games because they are bored. They kick the hornets' nest to get the buzz they are missing.

Who's a son of a bitch?

- **Think about a time when you played 'Now I've got you, you son of a bitch'. Why did you do it, and what does it tell you that you need to work on?** Maybe you saw a celebrity do something embarrassing, and you got a boost of 'Not so special now, are you?', which is a form of this game. Maybe you don't like another person at work, so you wait for them to make a mistake, so you have reason to complain about them. Did you play these games because you feared you weren't as good as them? If so, is it time to return to the sabotage chapter and work on your self-esteem or other beliefs that may affect how you feel about yourself? Or did you do it for another reason? No one will know your answer, so you are free to really take responsibility for your actions without judgement!

- **Consider a time when someone else has played 'Now I've got you' or another game with you. Identify the game and the potential causes and think about how you would address this situation if it were to arise again.** Everyone plays games and recognizing when we are being lured into someone else's drama is important for our sanity and our relationships. If they tried to pick a fight with you, and the moment you caved in, they seemed elated, were they playing 'Now I've got you, you son of a bitch' because they were angry about something totally unrelated that they were unable to tell you about? If so, if this happened again and you knew the person well, could you say to them, 'I feel like you are trying to lure me into an argument, but I am unsure why. Is something going on? Are you feeling angry for some reason? Rejected, maybe? I would love to know.' Or, as I said before, would you need to walk away? If someone started criticizing others around you, and tried to draw you into this undermining chat, were they playing blemish because something about that person made them uncomfortable? If so, if this happened again, could you use Socrates' three filters? Or could you expose the game by saying to them, 'I think that person's achievements are actually really impressive. So impressive it sometimes makes me feel insecure about myself, but then I remember that I can be happy for, and inspired by, others, and their success doesn't mean I am a failure.' Or: 'I don't want to fall into the trap of undermining other generations, as I often suspect this is driven by fear.' Or could you simply resist the game and say nothing at all?

Unsticking points

- Most games are driven by a desire for power, love and/ or care. However, boredom and bad habits could be reasons too.
- Some games can only be stopped by walking away.

Inverting the triangle

Getting unstuck in our relationships involves recognizing when and why we create the drama we experience. It involves getting to know the patterns of the people we spend time with too. While we can opt out of games and suggest to others their role in the conflicts they experience in life, we can only ever truly take responsibility for our own actions. Even if you do your best to step off the drama triangle, you may notice other people determined to continue to play the game, as they are not yet aware of the reasons why they do what they do. However, in my experience, most of the time, once one person in a relationship stops responding to the usual drama, it's as if they remove the fuel from the fire, and then, over time, the flames die down (more on how changing our behaviour affects the people around us in the next chapter).

We know that to get out of the drama triangle and the games we play, we need to approach the situation with self-awareness, compassion and curiosity. We need to recognize that we are okay AND other people are okay; we have the power to make decisions in our lives to suit ourselves AND so do the people around us. If we are often in the persecutor or rescuer role, we need to understand that we don't always know what is best for others, and supporting people to be themselves is not the same as telling them what to do. Once we've worked out where we are on the triangle, the next step is to consider inverting the triangle.

David Emerald, an American author and leadership coach, created 'the empowerment dynamic' to help us confidently opt out of the drama triangle. His model provides us with a route from victim to creator (giving us a chance to problem-solve), from persecutor to challenger (moving us from blaming others to asserting our needs and hopes constructively), and from rescuer to coach (preventing too much dependency on others to fostering mutual and healthy connections). The last part of this chapter will talk you through the steps to do this.

From victim to creator

When we want to become the creator, we must recognize that we are more capable than we realize. We must watch out for games, including 'Why don't you ...? Yeah, but ...' and 'Look what you made me do' and learn to ask for what we need. Shifting away from the belief we need others to rescue us and taking responsibility for ourselves can be downright scary. If this is you, think back to a time when you did something for yourself – a time you decided you wanted something and then did it. This is the empowering proof that you are perfectly able to decide what you want to do and what you will do.

Becoming the creator

- **Stop discounting yourself.** Repeat after me: *I am learning that I am more able than I have been giving myself credit for. Having support from others is great but I do not need to be rescued. I can take responsibility, action and risks.*
- **Return to your list of values, who you wish to be in the future, and your aimed-for habits.** Next to each hope for the future, write down the

---

steps you can take to achieve these goals, without waiting for someone else to step in. If this feels difficult, use the problem-solving technique from Appendix 2 to generate ideas. Next, write down everything that could get in the way of you being able to achieve these steps. Identify which of these blocks are self-generated (i.e. 'I just don't think I can do it') and which are real (i.e. you don't have enough money to start that thing). For the self-imposed blocks, challenge your thoughts, replace them with more balanced thoughts, and plan on how you will work around the blocks.

- **Notice negative self-talk and offer yourself compassion instead.** In Chapter 3, we discussed a simple way to start doing this, and where you could turn for more compassion-focused skills, but if you are really struggling with this, and think you could benefit from guided compassion-focused audios, I'd recommend looking up the work of Dr Kristin Neff, a leading voice in this field.

- **Build up your self-belief one step at a time.** Set up some small tasks that you can start today that help you see that you can do whatever you put your mind to. It is easy to logically believe that the more you face your fears, the easier you will find coping with setbacks and rejections. However, if you want to truly believe this with all your heart, it takes action and proving it to yourself over and over. If you are like Max, who always had his mum supporting his day-to-day life, you could write a list of the ways others support you and choose the one thing that sounds most manageable to try yourself. Or, if you are like Charlie and slip into victim mode when you haven't set boundaries in your relationships, decide on one thing you can say no to or delegate to another person today. The action you choose doesn't have to directly align with your future hopes, it only has to forge your belief that you have the power to do the things you wish to do in life. Once you find these initial steps easy, choose a slightly harder task and keep building. If you recognize you are avoiding doing these activities for reasons other than being stuck in the drama triangle, head back to Chapter 3 and implement the activities outlined there.

- **If someone else's behaviour is causing you to be in the victim role, you can still become the creator.** Could you address it with them? Could you tell them how you feel and what you want to happen? Could you put in a boundary? Could you leave them, should they keep hurting you?

From rescuer to coach

To become the coach, it's important to truly understand that other people − should they not have any factors that affect their capacity to make decisions in their best interests, and if you are not their carer, whose role it is to make decisions on their behalf − are equal adults who have the capacity to look after themselves and make their own mistakes. Taking a step back doesn't mean you are abandoning them and leaving them to struggle; it means respecting their ability to stand on their own two feet and allowing them to develop the tools to take responsibility for themselves.

If you are going to try this, beware of the games 'Why don't you ...? Yeah, but ...' and 'I was only trying to help' and consider what a good coach would do. Good coaches actively listen rather than jump in and give advice. They empower others to make moves without doing it for them and offer encouragement to keep going when mistakes are made and times get tough.

Becoming the coach

- **Repeat after me:** *I am learning that I can trust other adults to find their own way in this world. I don't need to guide them, as we are both okay. I am learning that I do not need to rescue others to be valued as a person.*
- **Look out for question marks.** When you think

---

someone is asking for help, consider whether the statement had a question mark at the end. If it didn't, don't join in! Alternatively, you can check: ask, 'Are you asking for help with that?' or 'That sounds really hard. Would you like to talk about it?'

- **If you are often brought in as the middleman during other people's conflict,** step out of the role by saying, 'That sounds tough. What do you think you will do?' If people try to keep you as a rescuer, tell them that the role isn't working for you and that you won't be in between them anymore. See what happens if you stop intervening. Sometimes it takes the rescuer to disappear in order for positive changes to occur.

- **Put boundaries around your time and energy and speak up.** Do this before you get frustrated with someone who isn't recognizing how much you are helping them. If you want support, make sure you ask for it. Don't assume others know that you are struggling, as they may be so used to you helping that they have no idea what you think or feel.

- **Recognize what drives your desire to rescue.** For example, you might try to support a friend to remove the anxiety you feel when you see them sad. In which case, you need to learn to manage your own emotional responses and then ask your friend if they would like support with how they feel.

From persecutor to challenger

To move from being a persecutor to a challenger, you need to look out for 'Look what you made me do' and 'Now I've got you, you son of a bitch'. And you need to learn how to assert your needs in an effective (i.e. non-aggressive) way. If you need to, there are ways to challenge other people's assumptions and behaviours without taking control of them or attacking their personhood. You can also take responsibility for your actions and your role in arguments without needing to also blame others.

Becoming the challenger

- **Repeat after me:** *I know it is compelling to criticize or be defensive, but there are more constructive ways to deal with my feelings.*
- **Take responsibility.** Recognize the moments you are feeling superior to and critical of others and apologize where necessary. And, do the same if you notice that you have deflected your guilt for an incident onto another. Apologizing doesn't make you weak. It shows you are a responsible adult who can take ownership of their behaviour, is willing to grow and wants to invest in the people around them.
- **Take care of your relationships.** Nitpicking is not the best way to get someone else to do something

---

and contempt is the fastest way to end a relationship. I know the persecutor role is compelling, but
do you want to be right? Or do you want to relate?

- **Focus on the real issue.** Try to work out what is
driving your tendency towards criticism and this
role. Address that instead of playing a game. For
example, instead of shouting, 'You never call me,
you're so self-obsessed,' you could say, 'I felt sad
when I didn't get a call today, it makes me worry
that you don't care.' This does not make you the
victim. It makes you an effective communicator.

- **Set your boundaries.** Learn to say no to things
you don't want to do without playing games or
criticizing others.

The final act

I am curious how it was for you to read this chapter and how
you are feeling now. Were you as defensive about it as I was
when I first came across this information? Are you ready to
step out of the dramas the people around you create, and
to walk off-stage when you notice you are cueing up other
people for their moment in the dramatic spotlight? Whatever
your answers, it's okay to not agree with what you read here
the moment you read it. It is okay if it takes time. Maybe you
will start to notice these little dramas playing out around you.
Maybe you won't right away. Maybe you will get right to it,

inverting that triangle. Maybe you will notice after a few days of getting it all right that you fall into the hypnotic trance of the drama triangle without realizing until it's too late. No problem if that's the case. You are human. You are fallible. Dramas are normal. You have time to fix them.

Chapter 5

History

*'History never repeats itself, but it does
often rhyme'*
—MARK TWAIN

Between 1918 and 1920, the Spanish flu killed an estimated 17–50 million people in Europe and the USA.[1] To end the pandemic, people had to wear masks, avoid physical contact and, if they were infected, quarantine – all measures that we are now sadly very familiar with.

The speed at which each country brought the epidemic under control correlated with the amount of quality information shared about effective management strategies, and how quickly those measures were put in place. The outbreak of the First World War impeded the spread of accurate information and action, partly due to disrupted information chains, but also because much information was censored, as some countries feared sharing the reality of their flu situation would make them appear weak when they needed to appear strong.[2] These factors meant that too little action was taken too late.

Fast-forward 100 years and experts in biodefence and related studies around the world feared that we were heading for another pandemic. They didn't know what kind of pandemic would arise, how deadly it would be or when it would occur ... they just knew one could and would come again sometime soon and that we needed to be prepared for it. So, why was everyone so underprepared when it finally did hit? We had generations of knowledge from other pandemics that could have helped us. Why did we go into it as if battling something totally new?

Multiple reasons. The obvious: few people understood the severity or virulence of the disease, because it was so hard to get hold of clear data. Quarantining and stay-at-home measures were not enacted in many countries until the pandemic had taken hold and hospitals were overrun – even in the nation that in 2019 was voted by the Global Health Security Index as the 'most prepared for a pandemic' in the world: the USA.

How did a country go from 'most prepared' to figuring it out as they went along? One of the major reasons is that, when administrations change, so do many of the staff in the different teams; computers are replaced and the data is wiped clean. George W. Bush had the National Strategy for Pandemic Influenza written when he was in office and built a team who would step into action should the worst happen. Barack Obama kept only part of the team, and temporarily built it back up during the swine flu. Donald Trump then replaced all the staff associated with biodefence, cutting budgets – including a $200 million early-warning programme created to identify potential pandemics.

When the coronavirus pandemic hit, the lessons from history had disappeared.

Why am I opening this chapter with this story? Because it perfectly illustrates the fact that patterns repeat across history and humans often don't always learn from their predecessors, or from their mistakes, meaning we tend to repeat them. In this final chapter, I am going to talk about the stuckness that arises because of patterns that play out across generations.

As you have seen, much of the stuckness we experience in our lives links to repeating patterns that no longer serve us. And, as you have also seen, repetition arises everywhere in our lives – in part as we are programmed to repeat actions to save time and energy and maximize our survival, and in part as we are drawn to what we know and act as if we are reading a script, assuming the roles that are most familiar to us. So how do we keep our hand out of the proverbial cookie jar and leave unhelpful scripts behind? We need to start by looking closer to home.

Family scripts

The feeling of following a script is something that the pioneering psychiatrist John Byng-Hall focused much of his work on. He proposed the notion of 'family scripts' – the patterns of behaviour we observe in the people around us in our formative years. These scripts are everywhere, from what mealtimes should look like (i.e. who sits where, what etiquette is used), how we treat others (i.e. how much effort we put into relationships, whether boundaries are implemented), how we should behave at certain ages (i.e. what you should wear and do), and how we should confront important issues (i.e. how to handle conflict).

Byng-Hall believed people tend to follow three main scripts:

- **The replicative script:** the patterns of behaviour and beliefs we learn from our family.
- **The improvised script:** a totally new pattern of behaviour that arises as we stumble into new territory and have to adapt, such as if there is a technological advancement and we have to learn a new way to engage with the world, or a pandemic or another situation in which we have never been before.
- **The corrective script:** when we consciously decide to act in a way that is different to what we were shown, generally as we didn't like what we saw and want to address the shortcomings of the script we learned.

Many of the scripts we carry are a blend of previous generations' scripts that have been passed along through bloodlines, close connections, family stories, and traditions such as music, recipes, religion, morals and myths. We are all the bearers of a legacy of scripts and find ourselves acting out those scripts, creating new intergenerational cycles of the same behaviour.

The scripts are sewn into our fabric, and they can pop up when we least expect it. Sometimes the repetition is subtle, as it doesn't look exactly as it did in the past. Maybe your family made you a specific meal when you were unwell (for me it was always dippy eggs and soldiers – thanks, Mum!) and now you find yourself heading to the kitchen when you are called upon to help someone in need. Maybe family members had affairs, and you find that you don't take romantic relationships seriously. This rings true with what Mark Twain said about history not repeating itself exactly, but rhyming; it feels familiar, and this in part is why we do it.

The scripts you keep alive

Name five (or more!) things you do that may replicate the actions and beliefs you saw growing up. Write your answers in the first column called 'Replicative scripts' in Appendix 4. Focusing on patterns in relationships, caring styles, health, work and money can be the best places to start if you are unsure.

Intergenerational trauma

Before we look at how to overcome and rewrite old scripts, we need to discuss one more thing. Intergenerational trauma, whereby someone else's pain can echo through us even though we didn't experience it first-hand, is becoming better understood in research and medicine. The idea that trauma could be passed through bloodlines was first considered when it was recognized that there was an overrepresentation in Canadian clinics of Holocaust survivors' grandchildren presenting with depression and PTSD symptoms.[3] Following that, clinics in other countries started noticing the same thing in the children of people who had lived through other mass genocides and wars.

Trauma is a response in the body when something overwhelms our ability to cope and causes a sudden and severe loss of safety. Two people could experience the same event, but only one might have a trauma response – it is the way our body reacts to the event rather than the event itself.

Trauma can be passed from one generation to the next by two potential mechanisms. If a caregiver is traumatized, it can affect how they are able to care for their baby. If they are dissociating (psychologically detaching from their environment), for example, they may not be able to show their children that the world is a safe place in which they can thrive, as they do not feel this themselves. This can mean that their child's nervous system develops to be in a state of high alert, without a good understanding of how to manage these emotions. If the caregiver is using alcohol to numb or regulate their pain, the child in their care may learn that this is the way to manage strong emotions. This may become the new 'normal' and be passed to the next generation in the same way.

The other route for intergenerational trauma is epigenetics, which is the study into how our environment interacts with our gene expression. Trauma can change the way our genes are expressed in our body and if the trauma is unresolved or happens during pregnancy, then these genetic changes can be passed on to the offspring.

Intergenerational trauma can mean that offspring come into the world primed for stress. From an evolutionary perspective, it could have been a hereditary superpower, as it meant that children were prepared for danger before they were born. Thousands of years ago, when humans were fighting for basic survival, it may have meant that new generations were hypersensitive to danger, and this hypervigilance may have helped them survive. These days, however, research suggests that intergenerational trauma can be responsible for many behavioural and social, but not cognitive, issues, such as depression and PTSD.[4]

Importantly, these epigenetic changes persist when off-spring are raised by someone who is not traumatized. I wanted to state this, as adoptive parents often feel like they have failed when their children struggle with their mental health. It can be helpful to know that it is not because they have failed, it is intergenerational trauma that is showing up, and this requires additional support from professional mental health services. If you believe there is intergenerational trauma in your family, consider reading *It Didn't Start with You: How Inherited Family Trauma Shapes Who We Are and How to End the Cycle* by Mark Wolynn. If you are experiencing depression, PTSD or another mental health issue that is causing you distress and is getting in the way of your quality of life, please seek support from a professional who knows how to make sense of your experiences.

Good news, though: intergenerational trauma can end with us, as long as we identify it and take time to address it. It's also reassuring to note that trauma isn't the only thing passed down through ancestral lines – resilience is, too.

Unsticking points

- Some of the reasons we are stuck link to patterns we repeat that started generations ago.
- Sometimes the patterns are learned from our environment; sometimes they may have been passed down through our DNA.

Flipping the script

How are you doing? This chapter is a little heavy, I know. This feels like a good point to reiterate that not everything is about the past. Not everything is about family or our beliefs. Many things happen spontaneously. Please don't assume that your past determines who you will be in the future, or that if your caregivers were traumatized that you will be too, or that if they did things you disagreed with, you now have no choice but to succumb to your fate. I hope by now you know that psychology is much more nuanced than immovable facts. You are not the *Titanic* heading inevitably towards the iceberg. In your story there may be no iceberg to face, as you may not have picked up the genetics or the scripts, but even if you did, there is plenty of time to pull that ship around.

The first step to breaking intergenerational patterns that take you away from who you wish to be in the future is to learn from the past, looking for patterns and ultimately deciding to do something different. This is what John Byng-Hall called the 'corrective script'. Maybe you were not allowed to watch TV or do anything fun as a child and now you decide that as an adult you will allow yourself as much fun as you can find. Or maybe your family kept secrets, so you practice transparency. Any time you decide to act in a way that is outside of what you have been taught, you are correcting a script.

One thing to bear in mind is that sometimes, when we try to do something different, we can come up against resistance. Maybe you were shot down by a family member armed to the teeth with reasons that your new idea won't work, or maybe you decided not to take the bait from that person who's always angling for a fight, and instead of this stopping them in their tracks, it only spurred them on. This resistance can happen for many reasons, but networks of closely connected people – friends, families, colleagues – often do not like change and feel most comfortable when everyone enacts their familiar patterns. Few people are aware they are doing this, but I see it happening all the time.

Remember Charlie and Max from the previous chapter? How easily Charlie had been pulled back into the rescuer role when she called Max and heard he was upset? Whenever we decide to act in ways that are out of the ordinary, resistance can occur. The moment other people are affected by our behaviour, the decision to change our patterns becomes more complicated. Change isn't impossible, of course, but it can sometimes take our social networks longer than we expect to get on board with the change, and to start seeing change as a good thing.

Unsticking point

- When you change your behaviour, others may resist. One option to manage this is to make your changes slowly – one step at a time. Another is to persist with your decision, knowing that, over time, other people will adjust.

Recognizing when you go off-script

- **Name five things you do that have nothing to do with your upbringing.** Put these in the 'Improvised scripts' column (in Appendix 4). Identify which of these scripts you would like to change. Circle them.
- **Name five things you do that are very different to what you saw growing up.** Put these answers in the third column called 'Corrective scripts' in Appendix 4.
- **List five behaviours/beliefs you don't like that you saw growing up.** Ask yourself: have you ever done any of these things? Why? Put these in the 'Replicative scripts' column. If you know you have purposefully avoided these behaviours, add what you have done instead to the 'Corrective scripts' column. Focusing on patterns in relationships, caring styles, health, work and money can be the best place to start if you are unsure.

- **Go through each of the scripts that you don't like. Who started that script?** Was it someone in the generation before you? Did they learn it from somewhere too? Did they behave that way because they thought it was right or because they didn't realize they were acting according to a script? Doing this will help create compassion rather than shame for any behaviour we repeat. If you aren't sure where the behaviour started, you could ask someone who may know earlier generations of your family and community.
- **Write down what a corrective script could be for each of the behaviours you don't like.** Don't spend too long on this, as we are going to address corrective scripts in more detail shortly.

Overcorrecting the script

Overcorrecting happens often when we flip a script we don't like and take it to a new extreme. A macro example of overcorrecting the script can be found in early twentieth-century America. In 1901, Carrie Nation, an activist in the American temperance movement, said that God came to her in her sleep and told her to smash up drinking holes. She listened. She wrapped rocks up in newspapers and threw them at saloon windows and the glasses inside. Five saloons later, she stepped up her weapon choice to a hatchet. Carrie Nation's 'hatchetations' laid waste to many saloons and made her notorious across the USA. She was arrested thirty times, and she toured the country giving lectures to raise awareness about the need for abstinence and prohibition.

Carrie Nation was such an icon of the temperance movement that she was nicknamed Carrie A. Nation. She was motivated not only by her religious belief that alcohol led to immorality, but by a very real problem in the USA at the time: soaring levels of domestic violence and alcohol-related crime and health conditions. Carrie had experienced such things first-hand: her late husband was often drunk, and died from pneumonia compounded by excessive drinking. Carrie may have taken extreme measures to bring about Prohibition, but in her eyes she was protecting men from the 'murder shops' (her name for saloons).

Prohibition finally came about in 1920, making the manufacture, transport and sale of alcohol illegal. At first it worked. There was a sharp fall in the number of people drinking. While it is impossible to get exact figures, the number of arrests for drunkenness, hospital admissions for alcoholic psychosis and deaths caused by cirrhosis of the liver and/or alcoholism recorded during that time suggest drinking rates dropped to about a third of where they were pre-Prohibition.[5]

But soon the Roaring Twenties got into full swing, and alcohol consumption rates rose to around 60–70 per cent of pre-Prohibition drinking levels. While this was still an improvement, new issues were arising. Since alcohol was no longer regulated, anyone could make it, and by any means, making it risky at best and lethal at worst. The underground market and consequent crime gangs boomed, and people were consuming stronger, transparent spirits to avoid being seen with more obvious substances like beer and wine.

Prohibition came to an end in most states in 1933 (although it took until 1966 in Mississippi), meaning that people could drink in legally licensed bars again, and alcohol was regulated and taxed. This is an example of overcorrecting the script from the history books, but we see instances of this in many of our day-to-day lives. When we decide to flip the script, even with the best of intentions, it might work for a while, but then we can often create new and more serious problems. And then, what happens? We end up in a cycle. One generation moves the dial, and the next moves it back, like a pendulum swing. Boom and bust is a familiar pattern to most of us: we sprain an ankle, we rest, and then we feel good, so we go for it, making up for lost time. The next day we can barely move.

Help, I'm stuck

'I have started having panic attacks and am so ashamed of it. I am so angry at myself for being so weak. I have always had it together – or at least I used to. I am pretty sure our family is cursed; mental instability is in our DNA. I thought I was the strong one. But now the panic is here, and my kids are struggling too. My mum passed it to me, and I'm passing it to them. What do I do?'

—LIZA, 38

Liza had grown up with a single parent who, as she remembers it, was often in floods of tears. Because of her mum's distress, she and her younger brother often had to figure out how to look after themselves and would spend hours trying to find ways to stem their mother's tears and ease her pain. It wasn't that Liza's mother was intentionally or consistently neglectful; most of the time her mum was present. It was just that Liza never knew when her mum would collapse into tears and need her help.

Considering these experiences, Liza made a promise to herself at a very early age that she would never allow emotions to get the better of her, so she wouldn't have to struggle like her mum did. She also vowed that she would never share how she felt so that no one would ever have to cope the way she and her brother had. She decided to flip the family script, and it worked. She worked as hard as she could in school, got married, and had children who never saw her struggle and never had to support her. She was the 'perfect' *I have it all together* mother. She was on top of everything. Until she started having panic attacks, that is.

Now that Liza was having panic attacks and her kids were struggling too, she assumed the issue was their DNA. They were all reportedly swinging from showing no emotions to total meltdown, which was often followed by shame and apology for having been so upset. She said that this resembled her mother's emotional state so closely it had to be genetic. Her conclusion was understandable, but through therapy we realized something else might be happening.

Liza wanted to ensure no one else had to be responsible for her feelings, but now her actions left her burdened by her own emotions. The panic attacks started because she was burned out and had no way to manage her increasingly frazzled emotional state. Liza had been so intent on hiding her emotions from her children that her kids had not learned what emotions were or how to manage them when they arose. They had also, it seemed, learned that showing emotions was considered a sign of weakness. This meant that when emotions did hit, they were ill-equipped to manage them. They became quickly overwhelmed and then ashamed that they had given in to their feelings. While we can't fully rule out DNA, it seemed that her children were exhibiting a common negative consequence of an overcorrected script.

Liza's intentions had been good, but just like a driver who spins the wheel against the skid as their car hits black ice, things had escalated and got worse. Fortunately, the consequences were rectifiable. After we addressed the panic attacks, Liza needed to understand which of her scripts were helping her, and which were causing new problems. She then needed to rewrite the corrective scripts that were causing the current predicaments. Having identified the overcorrected script: 'emotions are bad and must be avoided', she wrote a new statement that she wanted to share with her family: 'Emotions will arise. Emotions can be helpful. And, most importantly, emotions can be managed well.'

It's easy to write a new belief and believe in it in principle. It is more of a challenge to really take a belief to heart. The second step involved testing out Liza's theory so that the whole family learned to believe it.

We set up family sessions where each member could share what they knew about emotions, what they feared about them, and could ask any questions they had yet to have answered. Together we created a short and informal education session around emotions and anxiety with the kids, which their mum helped to lead, so that they knew she really did believe in this new way of thinking. At home, they practiced naming their emotions at regular intervals, and started a daily five-minute meditation practice as a family. Whenever Liza struggled, instead of shutting down, she would let her family know how she felt and what she was going to do about it. This included simple statements like: 'Today was stressful, I am going to have a bath and chill out' or 'I am feeling a bit nervous about the upcoming visit with the doctor, but I am talking it through with your dad and exercising to release the stress, so it's going to be okay.' Three months after they started this practice, a family friend died, and Liza allowed herself to cry in front of her family. The kids put their arms around her as her husband went to make her tea. She immediately felt better and recognized there were ways to share how you felt, without drowning everyone in your floods of tears and pain. Together, each of these activities proved to every member of the family that emotions were not to be feared and could indeed be managed well.

A quick side note: if you are struggling with your emotions, and don't know how to relate to them or manage them, I wrote all about this in *A Manual for Being Human*.

Unsticking points

- Overcorrecting old patterns can create new problems AND it can mean that the next generation ends up repeating the script that we so desperately wanted to avoid in the first place.

- Overcorrection can happen anywhere in our lives. For example, when we want to change a habit or a heuristic, we may say, 'I will never ever do X again,' but the expectation we set for ourselves is too high, so we fail. If you recognize you may have done this with your plans for new habits and heuristics, it's not too late to head back to them and make them a little more nuanced.

Have you overcorrected?

- **Ask yourself:** can you think of a time you made a conscious decision not to act in the way you saw someone else act when you were growing up? If yes, did your attempt at a 'corrective script' ever create new problems for you? Or has it ever led to a situation in which the original problem re-emerged, like it did for Liza? Did you see people who lived in chaos and decide to always have control over your life, and then go on to notice that your desire for control led to deep anxiety when something happened that you could not control? Did you vow never to be treated like a doormat by other people, as this is what happened in the relationships you saw growing up, and now notice your cool reserve means you have few friendships?
- **Go back to Appendix 4 and your new list of corrective scripts and consider whether you have**

> **created plans that are too polarized and need a
> little more nuance.** There will be more examples
> later if you need a little more information on what
> a middle way might look like.

'I told you so'

When we 'overcorrect', we don't simply run the risk of creating new problems; we can also give the people who disagree with us proof that they were right all along.

When Liza's panic attacks started, her mum said: 'Well, if you don't let the emotions in, they will overwhelm you. I did tell you that.' We see this all the time. A parent decides they won't be as strict as their parents were and let their children run free, potentially without enough boundaries. The original strict parent might then say: 'Your children are out of control' with a smug look on their face. On a larger scale, a government that worries about teenage pregnancies might manage this by avoiding the topic of sex in schools or directly telling young people that sex is bad. When stories in the news about teens watching violent porn circulate, the same people in charge might think, 'I knew young people can't be trusted to learn about sex; they have no self-control.' What they don't realize is that avoiding teaching factual information means teenagers will find another way to access the information.

The consequences of overcorrecting are bigger than a mere 'I told you so'. If future generations don't know how to take positive action, as they have only ever seen corrective action fail, we are in trouble as a society. They will feel paralyzed. When it came to Prohibition, Philip J. Cook, Professor Emeritus of Public Policy Studies and author of *Paying the Tab: The Costs and Benefits of Alcohol Control*, believes that the overcorrection paralyzed the nation, as the presumption that it was an all-out failure has meant that the federal government has felt unable to take actions to create a safer drinking culture (e.g. through increasing alcohol tax), meaning that there are 95,000 annual alcohol-related deaths in the USA and no real action taken to manage this.

I do not know the solution to societal drinking, but what I do know is that for us to make effective changes in our lives and in the world, we need to find an alternative to polarized action. We need a balanced middle path. Instead of swinging from being too strict to allowing your children to do whatever they want, we need to find ways to offer freedom and compassionate care while also instilling boundaries. Instead of swinging between no sex education whatsoever to giving young people full access to pornography and sexually explicit information, it is about engaging them in age-appropriate ways with the factual information that will help them make good choices. Recent research carried out by the Boston Public Health Commission found that directly talking to teenagers about pornography, sexual consent and healthy boundaries helped them to think critically and come up with ways they could prevent violence and stay safe.[6] So, there is always a way, even when it seems like there isn't.

Reclaiming nuance

• **Go back to your list of scripts in Appendix 4 and complete columns five and six.** Find any corrective scripts that you created that could be considered the polar opposite of your original script and write a more nuanced script instead. If you have taken too much control, could your new script be: 'I don't like chaos, but too much control is also leaving me feeling anxious. I will practice taking responsibility for what I can, but there are other coping skills that will help me to go with the flow and reduce anxiety going forward.' If you have pushed everyone away, maybe your new script could be: 'Relationships can be healthy. I can let people in and set boundaries to ensure people don't take advantage.' Write your answer in column five. Next, decide on the actions you will take to test out this belief. Will you need to learn a new skill like Liza and her family did? Will you need to risk doing something that feels scary in front of others? What will you do today to start this process? Write your answers in column six.

Unsticking points

- To prevent subsequent generations from reverting to the original unhelpful script, a more nuanced, modern approach is key.
- The solution is to find a more nuanced, moderate path.

Help, I'm stuck

'I'm scared about the future. I feel like the world is heading towards something bad. Climate change, prejudice, war – it all feels like it is just getting worse and worse, and I don't know what to do.'

—JOHN, AMY, GYNELLE, BEN, MAYOWA and HELGA ... The list of clients, friends, family members and people who connect with me online who have said an iteration of this comment is endless

I am hearing about these anxieties with increasing intensity in my clinic. It's so hard that, even with the incredible work of climate change scientists, racism and sexism educators, economists concerned about inequality, and many other experts in many other fields who have outlined how we could put an end to each of these issues, we don't seem to be making enough progress. We're all stuck.

Many believe that this stuckness is because not enough

225

people are educating themselves around the issues at hand and what needs to change. And that is, in part, very accurate. How can we overcome a climate crisis or racism if we deny its existence or if we never read about what we can do, and who we need to lobby to make real change happen? Believing people just needed to be 'educated' on topics, I wrote a chapter in my previous book dedicated to the effects of social injustice on mental health, and what actions could be taken to tackle not only the outcome of social injustice but to stop it from happening in the first place. The outcome of writing that chapter, plus the conversations I have in everyday life with people trying to change social issues, has shown me that education and interest are not the full picture.

The most obvious missing piece to this puzzle is that there are people who are extremely educated on a topic and who burn out or become overwhelmed by the news they come across each day, which sometimes leads to nihilism and a lack of ability to take the action that is necessary to make real change. This is why there is a movement to say that not only is it worth joining communities of people who are already working to solve the issues that are important to you so you can share their hope, but it can be helpful to minimize your news intake so that you don't consume too much bad news and become either overwhelmed or cynical. This way you will be able to use your energy to make positive change. And it is important to remember that some things feel worse now than ever simply because we have more access to the news. Devastating and violent things were happening pre-24/7 news cycles, we just didn't know about them, and data shows that the world (surprisingly) is actually safer now for the majority of its occupants than ever, which can be helpful to remember.

These ideas do not mean we should all stick our heads in the sand. They mean we need to create space between ourselves and the ongoing news cycle so that we don't burn out.

The less obvious missing piece of the puzzle comes in the shape of a hard-to-swallow pill. One that I had to choke down as I was researching this book and how on earth we get unstuck as a global population. As I said at the beginning of this chapter, if we are going to overcome our current stuckness as a society, we need to learn from history so we can stop repeating the same mistakes.

Lessons from history

1. Extreme polarization often impedes effective action and, at its most extreme, can put an end to democracy

For us to overcome important social issues, we need to be able to work together. Research looking at 'episodes of pernicious polarization' around the world found that since the 1950s, there have been fifty-two episodes of serious political polarization, and exactly half of those underwent significant decrease in the democratic rating of the country.[*][7] While our feelings of stuckness may not be as big as worrying that

---

* Research found a correlation between pernicious polarization and decrease in democratic rating. This does not mean that we can say there is a definitively causal relationship, but we can say there is a link.

our country will descend into a dictatorship, we must learn a lesson from history, which is that trouble stems from extreme polarization.

Some of the most important topics in the world right now are so polarizing, no conversation can be had around them. It is important we all have our views and our boundaries, but when we reach a point where we are totally unable to have conversations with anyone who doesn't have the exact same views as us, the divide only widens further.

When we have extremely polarized views, we end up in 'ad hominem' arguments, where we attack the person as if they are the problem, rather than addressing the actual problem. We position the other person as the villain and can become more obsessed with 'being right' than having a productive debate. We may also 'straw man', where we make an assumption about what the other person is saying and attack what we think we heard, rather than what was said. I'm sure everyone is guilty of doing this sometimes.

If we reject every person who disagrees with us (even on small differences), then we are missing opportunities to have conversations that could lead to real change. If we make assumptions about people who hold certain beliefs, we risk writing people off as someone they are not. When we do this, we run the risk of alienating the very people who may want to learn and be on our side. By making out that another person is 'bad' for their views and attacking them, we are likely to drive them away from our views rather than towards them. Shaming people rarely changes minds.

When extreme polarization occurs, we splinter into so many groups that no one is able to help each other. In the

Monty Python film *The Life of Brian*, the Judean People's Front and the People's Front of Judea are both groups of people fighting for Judea. Both groups hate the Romans and want to help the Jewish people, BUT the two groups hate each other due to interpersonal conflicts. Instead of uniting, they continued to be weakened by the divide. These scenes are funny in the film, but when they map directly onto reality, serious problems occur.

2. Extreme polarization leads to 'us' and 'them' divides

Research shows that empathy arises when we see that we have common ground with others. When we are extremely polarized and we separate ourselves into 'us' and 'them' groups, at best we start a drama triangle where we either try to rescue or demonize anyone outside of our group, and at worst, we start dehumanizing the people we consider different to us. There are too many examples across histories where people have been singled out for being different, and these perceived differences have led to significant atrocities.

We as a species have the highest levels of empathy for people we see as being in our personal networks. When these relationships are very strong, we have decreased empathy for people outside these groups. This wouldn't matter so much if we were not in such a polarized world, where we hold on to our beliefs so strongly that we see anyone who disagrees as the out-group. This is why polarized views can lead to dehumanizing others that don't fully agree with us. You only need to go on social media for a few minutes to see this. As we discussed in the case of Rose, who was struggling to decide about her Covid-19 vaccine, if someone makes a single error, or questions a held belief, they can end up on the receiving end of unending abuse, online and in real life. If we find out someone voted differently to us, we assume that they are 'stupid', 'naive' or 'dangerous'. We stop seeing nuance, which widens the divide even further.

3. When a group feels seriously disempowered, or afraid, there is a risk that they are more likely to believe fake news, make decisions that are not in their best interests, and follow extreme leaders

Scapegoats have been used throughout history to free the guilty from their sins and shame. In the lead-up to Brexit, immigrants were blamed for the NHS waiting lists, the lack of available jobs, and busy roads. They were the scapegoat. Some people were feeling disempowered and angry due to the state of the country, making them more likely to take the bait of scapegoats and fake news. Not only that, but when we fear a group, we are more likely to believe that the group has more members in it than is true, and we are more likely to believe that they are everywhere.[8] This is due to the exaggeration bias, which, as with all heuristics and biases, would have helped our ancestors stay safe – in this case by overestimating the threat of the enemy – but in our case, means that if we are not careful, we will fall prey to false and discriminatory narratives in the media.

Returning to the previous point, however, many people called Brexiteers racist, prejudiced and stupid. It isn't as simple as that. It isn't even as simple as the idea of an angry bunch who needed a scapegoat to rally against, or a fearful group who erroneously believed they were being invaded from every direction. For example, one arm of the campaign for Brexit targeted the fishing industry, saying that leaving Europe would increase their catch by hundreds of thousands of tonnes. This turned out to be untrue, but it was a compelling narrative taken on board by a lot of people that voted to leave the EU.

Right now, extreme polarization is making us more vulnerable to fake news and toxic factions of hatred. We are seeing an uptick in extremist groups, and the simplest explanation is that there are more sexist, racist and other types of prejudiced people than ever. A more nuanced view says this could be true AND it could also be true that there are more people who feel disempowered and angry, who are vulnerable to fake news. For example, one explanation behind incel groups is that men who have felt lonely and cast out take up the victim role (i.e. believe they have no options but to be angry), have been given a scapegoat (women) and a way to reclaim the feeling of power (by demonstrating the power they could wield against women).

I am not saying this so that we give empathy to people perpetuating hate. Absolutely not. I am saying this as we need to get clear about the psychology of some of the reasons people take extreme action should we want to overcome it. If we get caught up in polarized views, we lump people into one category and tend to alienate them, and miss out on important action points. And, should we notice we are feeling angry or afraid, we can use this information to ensure that we don't get tricked into perpetuating false information.

4. People are more likely to work together when the dire consequences of not doing this exist within living memory

Democracies and collective action thrive when people decide to put aside their differences to create harmony and work for collective health and wellbeing because they remember a recent disaster, war or atrocity.

I am not giving you these lessons from history to scare you. This is not where I say, 'Actually, ignore everything I said at the beginning. Grab the chocolate bar you have been avoiding, that bottle of wine you swore off, and get your ex on the phone, because we are going down and we may as well go out with a bang.' No, we have to talk about these things, and the lessons previous generations have learned, in order for us to create a society that can work together to create a safe future for everyone.

Whatever your beliefs, if we are going to move forward, we need each other and we need to work together.

Help, I'm stuck

> *'Am I saying I have to be kind to my racist uncle?' Am I*
> *saying I shouldn't get angry when people throw litter out their*
> *car window?' Am I saying I should meet an incel halfway?'*

—DR SOPHIE MORT

Throughout the book we have had examples from the people in my life, in my work and in the books I read. This one is from me. This chapter has been the hardest for me to come to terms with. When I read the research that I have shared with you, I fell into every trap they said was a consquence of polarized thinking. I engaged in straw-manning and ad hominem thinking styles; I called the writers assholes with secret agendas trying to talk down people who were fighting to make change in the world. I read each article as if it said, 'Don't get so worked up', 'Everyone should just be friends and if we can make sense of other people's behaviour, then we shouldn't get angry' – all of which left me worked up and angry! Then I took a breath. And another. I let the emotion pass as I, like you, know about confirmation bias, the affect heuristic, and all the other ways in which our brain can trick us into getting carried away. Then, I returned to mulling over what I had read. And I realized . . .

Saying we need to consider polarization and the way we interact with others is not saying don't have conviction. It is saying: remember to take conviction and draw lines when it is necessary. Much of the time it means recognizing when you make assumptions about someone, and then remembering fundamental attribution error (the tendency to assume that other people's actions reflect their character when ours can be explained by context), the halo effect and confirmation bias. It means pausing and then asking, 'What could I be missing?' Then, once you have done that, deciding whether the line needs to be drawn.

Nuance and middle ground are going to help us decrease polarization. I don't mean we all have to say, 'I will meet you exactly halfway.' I don't mean saying yes to things that clearly need you to say no. I don't mean not having an opinion. I don't mean befriending your local misogynist. I don't mean agreeing that climate change doesn't exist when you know full well it does. I mean we need to find somewhere that considers that there is a large grey area between two black-and-white choices, and that somewhere in there likely lies the way forward. For me, that means addressing statements that come across as prejudiced, but not assuming that the person is bad or that all of their thoughts and beliefs are prejudiced. It means getting curious about why someone would deny the evidence that the world is warming up. It means wholeheartedly having hard opinions about people who harm, while also seeing that governments and societies who want to stop that harm being perpetuated in the future need to consider how to reach those communities. It means holding two opposing views in mind at the same time, with the hope that in the murky middle, we will find something that can progress a conversation.

Sometimes finding common ground, nuance and a middle way is easy. You decide to notice when you want to push away anyone who has a slightly different belief to you and actively stay open to what they are saying instead, seeing this as an opportunity to find out if this person is 'as bad' as you assume they are, or whether you can learn from and help each other.

Sometimes finding middle ground will involve over-correcting and then finding your way, like Liza did. This is similar to the ideas of dialectics put forward by philosophers like Kant, Hegel and Marx (among others), who said that the progression of ideas often follows the path of thesis (a new idea is proposed), antithesis (an opposing or contradictory argument is made) and synthesis (a third approach or idea is reached, resolving the tension between the thesis and antithesis, creating a path forward). Synthesis isn't always a mix of each idea, or a compromise, but can be a totally new idea entirely, and as progress rarely ever stops, synthesis often becomes the new thesis that starts the next cycle of conversation. Progress is rarely linear, and that's okay. If you are reading this thinking about a clear overcorrection you may have made, that's normal. It's trial and error and you will likely find a way that works for you soon.

The middle ground is not a new idea, but I think that nowadays we see it as 'unradical'. However, middle ground is often the most radical view of all. It says I have looked at the evidence, really looked, and am willing to not throw the baby out with the bath water but look for a more nuanced way of thinking that may actually help us move forward.

And importantly, middle ground is not always the way to go. There are certain situations in which middle ground is wholly unacceptable. Some things are simply wrong, bad, etc. For example, rape and murder are always bad. And let's say you offer someone a curious conversation about their views, and they are determined to pick fights, spread hate, or hurt you or others – middle ground, be gone. It is time to draw a line in the sand. Set your boundary, say your piece, walk away or whatever works for you. Not all situations can be depolarized. And they are not meant to be. But, for us to truly get unstuck, we must consider what we have learned throughout this book.

Each of us err. Each of us, from time to time, gets stuck due to our habits, heuristics, sabotage, games, and history. More often than we would like to admit, we: enact behaviours we wish we had let go of long ago; make snap judgements about each other based on singular facets and look for information that confirms only our beliefs, avoiding or shaming anyone who disagrees, irrespective of whether we are correct in doing so; take the easy route, avoiding discomfort; put other people in roles that they don't choose, and blame others instead of owning our parts; and make choices that have consequences that are a little more extreme than intended. If we know that we do this, then we need to recognize that the people in our lives do these things too. If we want to get unstuck in our lives, we need to give ourselves grace. And we need to take responsibility for our actions. This is the same for the people around us. Because, as I said before, if we want to get unstuck as a population, we are going to need each other.

Unsticking points

- There are lessons from history that can help us reach a brighter future.
- When people do not listen to each other, terrible things can happen. Having strong opinions, fighting for collective change, etc., is a good thing. However, at present, some of our best efforts are causing more of a divide, which is hampering change.
- Sometimes we need to focus our efforts on changing the systems, and the media that feeds our polarization, fear and misinformation, rather than fight each other.

When two things are true

- Try using 'both/and' as a way of holding opposing positions in mind at the same time. For example, it is both true that I was overwhelmed by my parents' emotions and also true that I must learn to feel and cope with mine and show this to my children in order for them to gain emotional resilience. It is true that the specific comment I heard may mean that person holds views that I can't get on board with, and it is also true that I may be wrong, and this conversation is an opportunity for growth for both of us.

- Bring to mind a time when you held a very different view to your current belief system. How did you change this opinion? Did you find middle ground easily or did you overcorrect? Did that opinion mean that you were a certain person – maybe a 'goodie' or a 'baddie' – or can you see that you have more shades of grey than that, and might have views that may sometimes need updating? Can you bring to mind an opinion that you are grateful to have been educated about rather than shamed for? Is there a strong opinion you have that, as you read this, you consider you may want to find middle ground for?

- Bring to mind something that someone else did or said that was at odds with your belief, that caused you to make assumptions about them as a person, and to write them off. Looking back at that time, is there something that you might have missed? An opportunity to find out more about them and to have a useful conversation? Did you go back to them and have that conversation at a later date? This exercise isn't trying to make a specific point. It is to get you thinking about your own experiences of some of the topics proposed in this chapter so that you can come to your own decisions.

- Decide on one thing, or one occasion, where you are pleased that you stuck to your guns during a discussion. Ask yourself why you are pleased that you didn't try to find middle ground here. Is it because you were discussing something that felt non-negotiable? What does it tell you about what you think is important in life?

I am asking you to do this as your final task because books like this can seem like they are constantly telling you what you are doing wrong and what you need to change. They rarely focus on the fact that you know yourself better than any author can know you, and that you are not a constant self-development project, but someone who likely already has a good grasp on who they are, is already doing really important acts that align with their values, and is likely quite fantastic just as they are. This final question is therefore to reiterate that even though learning more about yourself and how you can get unstuck in life is important, there are so many times in your life where you have already stood up for what matters to you. Moments where you have already made great choices and taken action when you needed to. Moments where the simplest solution to feeling unstuck is celebrating what is already here rather than pining after what is yet to be.

A final note to you

Phew. We made it! How are you doing?

This book has announced a million and one ways in which we can end up stuck. And it has shown at points that we are often on a never-ending loop of repeating the past. But there are a few things that we need to remember: 1) this is not because there is something wrong with us; these things are normal; we just need to understand them in order to make sure they don't get in the way of our lives, and 2) you now have the knowledge to identify your patterns, as well as the many things that may get you stuck.

In addition, I want to ensure you go away with this message: we humans have amazing and helpful abilities. Abilities such as habits and heuristics, that help us save energy so that we can focus on survival and other important aspects of life. Abilities such as sabotage and the drama triangle, that help us stay safe from shame or breaking the rules we believe need to be kept. And we can recognize what's not working for us, and create new rules and actions for ourselves that mean we can correct any issue we find ourselves in.

Unfortunately, as we have learned across this book, each of these abilities leaves us at risk of being worse off should we not be careful. Bad habits can ensue. Biases can lead us to vaginal burns(!). Sabotage and drama can provide evidence that our worst fears are true. And overcorrecting can lead us to new problems.

When people say, 'This is just who I am; I can't change,' they are either not yet at the point where they are ready for change, or they have had an experience of trying to make change and failing, or they simply haven't seen change done. Even in the cases where change seems impossible, there is usually something we can do to change our relationship to the thing we are struggling with.

You now have the ability to recognize where each of these issues can arise. You have the tools to get on top of these issues: mindfulness to help you get aware, which is the first step to making any meaningful change in life; action steps to challenge whichever form of stuckness is your personal bête noir; and, hopefully, a little more compassion for the reasons you may engage in each and any of the topics discussed here.

Compassion plus responsibility is the perfect recipe for making change in life. It keeps us out of old habits as it helps dampen the stress response and gives us hope that change can happen. It keeps us out of heuristics as it reminds us to hold space for other people's opinions and stops us from beating ourselves up for making imperfect decisions. It keeps us out of sabotage as it shows us we don't need to avoid the things we fear. It keeps us out of drama as it stops us from playing the many faces of the victim. And, it says if I did overcorrect, I will now find a way forward. It recognizes that progress may be slow, but that, like the tortoise, slow and steady wins the race.

I am not saying it will be easy. I am saying that if we come together to help each other make the changes we need, we will succeed. Collective action could include holding each other accountable for our new habits; challenging our tendency towards groupthink and confirmation bias; supporting each other to face our fears so we don't self-sabotage; engaging in honest conversations so we don't play games; and finding common ground so that we can tackle the serious threats that all generations tend to face. Yes, we need to look at our own actions that keep us stuck, but to really unstick ourselves and future generations to come, we need each other.

Before I let you go back to living your life, I want to reiterate one more thing on the winding nature of change and the fact that sometimes progress will be made and then a setback will occur. When this happens, and it likely will, you must remember it is all part of the process, rather than a sign that you are back at square one. It will take time for you to break the habits you no longer wish to engage in.

If you try something from this book and you notice a setback, remember the furry little mice we talked about in Chapter 1. The ones who won their place under the heat lamp, not due to strength but perseverance. Repetition is your friend, and with it on your side, you will finally feel un-stuck.

Dr Soph x

Further reading

If you want to learn more about habits, further reading could include:

Atomic Habits by James Clear

Nudge by Thaler and Sunstein

If you want to learn more about the stages of motivation and how to move through them:

Changing to Thrive: Using the Stages of Change to Overcome the Top Threats to Your Health and Happiness by Prochaska and Prochaska

If you want to go into depth about heuristics and biases:

Thinking, Fast and Slow by Daniel Kahneman

The Undoing Project: A Friendship that Changed the World
by Michael Lewis

If you want to learn more about self-criticism and
self-compassion:

A Manual for Being Human by Dr Sophie Mort!

*Self-compassion: The Proven Power of Being Kind to
Yourself* by Kristin Neff, PhD

If you want to learn more about self-esteem:

The Six Pillars of Self-Esteem by Nathaniel Branden

If you want to learn more about games:

Games People Play by Eric Berne

If you want to learn more about intergenerational trauma:

*It Didn't Start with You: How Inherited Family Trauma
Shapes Who We Are and How to End the Cycle* by
Mark Wolynn

Resources

Appendix 1

Choose your habits

Write down who you would like to be in the future (choose five value-driven words, such as 'kind, healthy, committed, present, free'):

_____

_____

_____

_____

_____

Write down what you would like to be doing in the future (choose five goals):

_____

_____

_____

_____

_____

If you can't yet answer those questions easily, complete the values activity found on page 93 in Chapter 2.

Complete the following columns:

Column 1	Column 2	Column 3	Column 4	Column 5
Habits that you already do that are in line with the person you wish to be.	Habits that take you away from being who you wish to be.	Cues that cause you to engage in these 'bad' habits (some will be visual; some will be physical sensations). After completing this column, circle the ones you can and will remove.	The reward or resolution this habit achieves (i.e. what purpose does the habit serve, does it get rid of a craving? Does it get rid of boredom?)	The new activity that could achieve the same resolution and/ or takes you towards who you wish to be. (Write down the new activity, then break it down into smaller chunks if it is a big task.)

CHOOSE YOUR HABITS

Column 6	Column 7	Column 8	Column 9	Column 10	Column 11
Good habits you would like to develop. (Write this list on a grid line lower than the line you last filled out in column five.)	The cues you will have to add into your day to trigger new behaviour.	Rewards you will set up for that new behaviour.	When you will do these new actions (what time of day, and before or after what other activity you already engage in).	Who you will tell about your new actions and how they will support you.	What you will do if you slip back into an old habit.

Appendix 2

Solve your problems

1. Write down the problem you are trying to solve, or the decision you are trying to make (e.g. your job is not going well, or your boss is a micromanager).

   _____

   _____

   _____

   _____

   _____

   _____

2. **In column one, write as many possible solutions as you can think of.** Make sure there are least FIVE possible solutions to that problem without thinking about whether they are possible or not. These may not come to you easily. You may have to ask others what they would suggest as solutions, or,

alternatively, ask yourself what you would suggest to a friend in the same situation. Notice any temptation to ignore a potential solution at this stage. All possibilities, no matter how unlikely, should be listed here.

3. **Add at least ONE totally ridiculous solution.** Something that makes you laugh. This helps relax us a little and helps us recognize that there is almost always something we can do when we face a problem.

4. **In columns two and three, write down the pros and cons of each item.** Really think this through. Take your time. Make sure you write at least one pro and one con. Include what other people would tell you are the pros and cons in these too.

5. **Circle the choice that feels most likely/manageable.** Having read through the pros and cons, which one do you feel seems most realistic for you to try? You may at this point want to combine a couple of the possible solutions, making a blended solution.

6. **Decide how you would put that into practice.** Be specific. Write down what you will do, when you will do it and what you will need to be able to do that thing.

7. **Do that thing!**

8. **Review the outcome.** Take time to come back to this activity. Write down what happened. Write down whether it was the outcome you wanted or different to that. Decide whether you have met your need or not. If not, try another solution.

SOLVE YOUR PROBLEMS

Possible solutions	Pros of this solution	Cons of this solution	What you will try first (and how and when you will try it, and what you will need to do in order to try it)	How it went

Appendix 3

Challenge your fears

These steps are adapted from a psychological model called Cognitive Behavioural Therapy. If you are really struggling with fear or anxiety, and find that completing this exercise is not enough to help manage your fears, consider getting support from a therapist who specializes in CBT.

1. **Write down the fear that is keeping you stuck** – e.g. 'Something will go wrong if I open myself up to a new relationship' or 'I am bad at everything I try'.

    _____

    _____

    _____

    _____

2. **Put the fear on trial:** if the fear thought is so strong it makes it hard for you to see the evidence that

challenges the fear thought, you can ask other people to help you with this task.

- In column one, list the evidence that supports your fear thought. E.g. 'The person I dated recently cheated on me' or 'I didn't get the job I just applied for'.
- In column two, list the evidence that challenges your fear thought. E.g. 'The previous three people I dated treated me well, and even though I was sad when those relationships ended, no one got truly hurt' and 'I have lots of friends who are kind, supportive, and who have never hurt me'. Or 'When I didn't get the job, they said it was because the other person had two more years' experience than me, so maybe what I interpreted as proof I am bad at everything and others agree, isn't that at all' and 'Every skill I have right now, including writing and reading, were once tasks I didn't know how to do, but now I can do them, so maybe I am not bad at everything I try'.
- In column three, write a new, more balanced belief that reflects both sides of the evidence. E.g. 'Dating can lead to painful feelings but not all people hurt you – in fact, most of the people I meet are kind, supportive and make me believe in the value of taking risks and getting to know others.' Or, 'Sometimes I worry I am bad at everything, when in reality, what I interpret as proof of this is usually explainable in other ways and I have many examples of pushing through the early stages of trying a new activity and succeeding in the end.'

CHALLENGE YOUR FEARS

Evidence for your fear	Evidence that challenges your fear	A new balanced belief

3. **Follow the 'what ifs?' to the end.** This time, instead of challenging the fear, we are going to play along with our fears' tendency to get us stuck in a rabbit hole of 'what if this or that went wrong'. This exercise is important, because anxious thoughts such as 'what if X happened' usually stop us in our tracks and make us forget to ask what we would actually do should our worst fear arise. By following the 'what ifs' to the end, we can remove some of the sting created by the fear.

• Write down your fear thought in 'what if' form. I.e. what if (insert your fear thought here) happened/was true? What if I meet someone and they hurt me? What if I try this and everyone laughs at me?

_____

_____

_____

_____

_____

• Ask yourself, 'What would I do if that really did happen?' Write down exactly how you would manage that scenario. E.g. 'I would be really upset and embarrassed and possibly rush home and have a good cry. It would prove my worst fears were true all along.'

_____

_____

_____

_____

_____

_____

- Ask yourself, 'What would I do then?' E.g. 'I would probably sob for a week, spend a lot of time in bed and call a friend to ask for support.'

_____

_____

_____

_____

_____

- Ask yourself, 'And then what?' E.g. 'I would probably feel better for a while and then feel bad again.'

_____

_____

_____

_____

_____

- Ask yourself, 'What would I do then?' E.g. 'I would write a list of what I think went well and didn't go so well so I could use it for future attempts. I would make sure I exercised and do other activities that I know help me to manage my emotions, then I might consider trying again.'

_____

_____

_____

_____

_____

_____

- Keep asking yourself what you would do until you can't go any further. E.g. 'I would eventually get over the pain/embarrassment and start dating again/trying new things again.'

_____

_____

_____

_____

_____

- Once you get to this point, ask yourself: 'So would it be scary if this happened?' And then ask yourself, 'But would I survive it?' The answer to both of which will likely be yes.

4. **Plan how you will test out your new beliefs.** Now that you have a more balanced approach to your fear thought, and a plan for what you would do even if the worst outcome happened, it is time to set up a behavioural experiment that either slowly exposes you to the situation you fear or that tests out your new fear belief. If you remember Jia from Chapter 3, you already know that the best way to overcome fear of rejection is to put yourself in the line of rejection repeatedly, building from the least scary rejection

example you can think of, up to the scariest. This strategy works for most areas of our lives.

- Following exercises 1 and 2, you may want to write a totally new belief, such as 'rejection and failure don't always happen and even when they do, they are survivable'. Write this new belief or the belief you want to test out here:

_____

_____

_____

_____

_____

_____

- Ask yourself, 'What is the least scary thing I could do today to test out my fear?' E.g. if you fear rejection, will you do as Jia did and ask a stranger to do something totally random for you and see what they say? If you fear failure, will you cook something tonight and burn a small part of that meal on purpose and not tell anyone what or why you have done it, in order to see how others respond?
- Ask yourself, 'What is the next least scary thing I could do to test out my fear?'
- Ask yourself this at least five more times, until you have written a list of at least seven steps you can take to test out your fears.

List your seven steps to face your fear here:

1. The least scary thing I will do is:

   _____

   _____

   _____

   _____

   _____

   _____

2. The next thing I will do is:

   _____

   _____

   _____

   _____

   _____

   _____

3. The next thing I will do is:

   _____

   _____

   _____

   _____

   _____

   _____

4. The next thing I will do is:

   _____

   _____

   _____

_____
_____
_____

5. The next thing I will do is:

_____
_____
_____
_____
_____
_____

6. The next thing I will do is:

_____
_____
_____
_____
_____
_____

7. The next thing I will do is:

_____
_____
_____
_____
_____
_____

Write down when you will do the first step here:

_____

and then move to the next step.

8. **Do the experiment.** Before you do it, complete part A of the form below. After you have done the experiment, complete part B. Do this for each step on your list.

A.

Today I am going to do *(write your activity here)*

_____
_____
_____
_____
_____

I am doing it to test the belief that *(write the belief you are testing here)*

_____
_____
_____
_____

At present I have *(write down how much you believe the above thought out of 100 here)* _____ per cent faith in the belief I am testing.

When I do this test, I think that *(write down any worries here)*

_____

_____

_____

_____

_____

I will look after myself during this experiment by *(write down what measures you will take to make this test manageable, such as 'I will take a friend with me to do this', 'I will meet a friend afterwards to debrief'.)*

_____

_____

_____

_____

_____

B (complete afterwards)

During the test *(write down what happened, how you felt, and what surprised you)*

_____

_____

_____

_____

From this test I learned *(write down what you can take away from this experiment; it doesn't all have to be 'good stuff', maybe it was embarrassing but you lived to tell the tale)*

_____

_____

_____

_____

_____

I now have *(write down how much you believe the above thought out of 100 here; it may or may not have changed)* _____ per cent faith in my new belief.

The next test I will do is *(write here whether you will move to step 2 of your plan to face your fears or whether you will need to do step 1 a few more times before you feel ready to progress)*

_____

_____

_____

_____

Repeat all the steps as necessary. You may notice that new fears crop up as you do more challenging tasks. That is okay. There is no need to rush. If new fears arise, head back and put the new fears on trial, then follow the what ifs to the end, and set up your experiment to face your new fears and put your new beliefs to the test.

Appendix 4

Flip your scripts

1. Write down your replicative, improvised and corrective scripts as set out in Chapter 5 on page 208.

As a quick reminder:

- **Replicative scripts** are the patterns of behaviours that mirror what you saw growing up.
- **Improvised scripts** are the patterns you made up for yourself as you were not taught.
- **Corrective scripts** are the patterns of behaviours/ beliefs that you used to replace behaviours/beliefs you saw and didn't like.

2. Circle the scripts you no longer wish to engage in as they take you away from who you wish to be.
3. Complete column four by asking yourself who the

first person was to engage in these behaviours and to have these beliefs.

4. Write down a new corrective script to manage any script you have circled but that at present doesn't have a corrective script.

5. Ask whether any corrective scripts are extreme, and then complete column five.

6. Write down what you will need to do to test out your new script, as well as what skills you will need to learn.

Column 1	Column 2	Column 3
Replicative scripts	Improvised scripts	Corrective scripts

(UN)STUCK

Column 4	Column 5	Column 6
Where did each script that you don't like start? Is there someone in your family tree or social network who did this? Why?	What would be a more nuanced corrective script?	What will you have to do to test out this new script?

Notes

1 Deery, H. A., Di Paolo, R., Moran, C., Egan, G. F., & Jamadar, S. D., 'The older adult brain is less modular, more integrated, and less efficient at rest: a systematic review of large-scale resting-state functional brain networks in aging', *Psychophysiology*, 60, e14159 (2023).
2 Neal, D. T., Wood, W., and Quinn, J. M., 'Habits – A Repeat Performance', *Current Directions in Psychological Science* 15, no. 4 (2006): 198–202.

Chapter 1: Habits

1 Job, V., Dweck, C. S., and Walton, G. M., 'Ego Depletion – Is It All in Your Head?: Implicit Theories About Willpower Affect Self-Regulation', *Psychological Science* 21, no. 11 (2010): 1686–1693.
2 Lally, Phillippa, van Jaarsveld, Cornelia H. M., Potts, Henry W. W., and Wardle, Jane, 'How are habits formed: Modelling habit formation in the real world', *European Journal of Social Psychology* 40, no. 6 (2010): 998–1009.
3 Malvaez, Melissa, and Wassum, Kate M., 'Regulation of habit formation in the dorsal striatum', *Current Opinion in Behavioral Sciences* 20 (2018): 67–74.
4 Davey, J. and Jack, V., 'Crunch time in Britain as even beloved crisps in short supply', Reuters, 5 November 2021. https://www.reuters.com/business/retail-consumer/crunch-time-britain-even-beloved-crisps-short-supply-2021-11-05/

5 Moss, M., *Hooked: How Processed Food Became Addictive* (Ebury Publishing, 2021).

6 Gardner, S., and Albee, D., 'Study focuses on strategies for achieving goals, resolutions', *Press Releases* 266 (2015), https://scholar.dominican. edu/news-releases/266

7 Zhou, T., et al., 'History of winning remodels thalamo-PFC circuit to reinforce social dominance', *Science* 357, no. 6347 (2017): 162–168.

8 Phillips, L. A., and Gardner, B., 'Habitual exercise instigation (vs. execution) predicts healthy adults' exercise frequency', *Health Psychology* 35, no. 1 (2016): 69–77.

9 Wilson, R. C., Shenhav, A., Straccia, M., and Cohen, J. D., 'The Eighty Five Percent Rule for optimal learning', *Nature Communications* 10, no. 1 (2019): 1–9.

10 Adolph, K. E., et al., 'How do you learn to walk? Thousands of steps and dozens of falls per day', *Psychological Science* 23, no. 11 (2012): 1387–1394.

11 Eyal, Nir, 'Forming New Habits: Train to be an Amateur, Not an Expert', *Nir and Far*, 17 February 2021, https://https://www.nirandfar. com/train-to-be-amateur-not-expert/

12 Kappes, H. B., and Oettingen, G., 'Positive fantasies about idealized futures sap energy', *Journal of Experimental Social Psychology* 47, no. 4 (2011): 719–729.

Chapter 2: Heuristics

1 Van Vugt, M., and Schaller, M., 'Evolutionary approaches to group dynamics: An introduction', *Group Dynamics: Theory, Research, and Practice* 12, no. 1 (2008): 1–6.

2 Hare, B., 'Survival of the Friendliest: Homo Sapiens Evolved via Selection for Prosociality', *Annual Review of Psychology* 68, no. 1 (2017): 155–186.

3 Robert, M., 'Second-Degree Burn Sustained After Vaginal Steaming', *Journal of Obstetrics and Gynaecology Canada* 41, no. 6 (2019): 838–839.

4 Kluger, J., 'Accidental Poisonings Increased After President Trump's Disinfectant Comments', *TIME*, 12 May 2020, https://time. com/5835244/accidental-poisonings-trump/

5 Smyth, S. M., 'The Facebook Conundrum: Is it Time to Usher in a New Era of Regulation for Big Tech?', *International Journal of Cyber Criminology* 13, no. 2 (2019): 578–595.

6 Romm, T., 'Pro-Beyoncé vs. Anti-Beyoncé: 3,500 Facebook Ads Show the Scale of Russian Manipulation', 10 May 2018, *Washington*

Post, https://www.washingtonpost.com/news/the-switch/wp/2018/
05/10/here-are-the-3400-facebook-ads-purchased-by-russias-online-
trolls-during-the-2016-election/

7 Goszczyńska, M., and Rosłan, A., 'Self-evaluation of drivers' skill:
a cross-cultural comparison', *Accident Analysis & Prevention* 21, no. 3
(1989): 217–224.

8 Cooper, A. C., Woo, C. Y., and Dunkelberg, W. C., 'Entrepreneurs'
perceived chances for success', *Journal of Business Venturing* 3, no. 2
(1988): 97–108.

9 Johnson, D. D. P., *Overconfidence and War: The Havoc and Glory of
Positive Illusions* (Harvard University Press, 2004).

10 Alsabban, S., and Alarfaj, O., 'An Empirical Analysis of Behavioral
Finance in the Saudi Stock Market: Evidence of Overconfidence
Behavior', *International Journal of Economics and Financial Issues* 10, no. 1
(2020): 73–86.

11 Stone, C., Mattingley, J. B., and Rangelov, D., 'On second thoughts:
changes of mind in decision-making', *Trends in Cognitive Sciences* 26,
no. 5 (2022): 419–431.

Chapter 3: Self-Sabotage

1 Hirt, E. R., McCrea, S. M., and Kimble, C. E., 'Public Self-Focus
and Sex Differences in Behavioral Self-Handicapping: Does Increasing
Self-Threat Still Make it "Just a Man's Game?"', *Personality and Social
Psychology Bulletin* 26, no. 9 (2000): 1131–1141.

2 Ibid.

3 Tully-Wilson, C., Bojack, R., Millear, P. M., Stallman, H. M., Allen,
A., and Mason, J., 'Self-perceptions of aging: A systematic review of
longitudinal studies', *Psychology and Aging* 36, no. 7 (2021): 773–789.

4 Linscott, R.N., *Complete Poems and Selected Letters of Michelangelo*, trans.
Creighton Gilbert (Random House, New York, 1963, 1965): 218.

Chapter 5: History

1 Jordan, D., Tumpey, T., Jester, B., 'The Deadliest Flu: The Complete
Story of the Discovery and Reconstruction of the 1918 Pandemic Virus',
Centers for Disease Control and Prevention, https://www.cdc.gov/flu/
pandemic-resources/reconstruction-1918-virus.html

2 Little, B., 'As the 1918 Flu Emerged, Cover-Up and Denial Helped
It Spread', 26 May 2020, History, https://www.history.com/
news/1918-pandemic-spanish-flu-censorship

3 Rakoff, V., Sigal, J. J., and Epstein, N. B., 'Children and families of concentration camp survivors', *Canada's Mental Health* 14, no. 4 (1966): 24–26.

4 Alhassen, S., Chen, S., Alhassen, L., et al., 'Intergenerational trauma transmission is associated with brain metabotranscriptome remodeling and mitochondrial dysfunction', *Communications Biology* 4, no. 783 (2021).

5 Miron, J. A., and Zwiebel, J., 'Alcohol Consumption During Prohibition', *American Economic Review* 81, no. 2 (1991): 242–247.

6 Rothman, E. F., Daley, N., and Alder, J., 'A Pornography Literacy Program for Adolescents', *American Journal of Public Health* 110, no. 2 (2020): 154–156.

7 Somer, M., McCoy, J. L., and Luke, R. E., 'Pernicious polarization, autocratization and opposition strategies', *Democratization* 28, no. 5 (2021): 929–948.

8 Ponce de Leon, R., Rifkin, J. R., and Larrick, R. P., '"They're Everywhere!": Symbolically Threatening Groups Seem More Pervasive Than Nonthreatening Groups', *Psychological Science* 33, no. 6, (2022): 957–970.